HOW TO GET YOUR ACT TOGETHER

'Suki Sandhu and Felicity Hassan make a compelling case
why creating more diverse and inclusive workplaces is everybody's
business. *How to Get Your Act Together* is a must-read
and a powerful call to seize the opportunity that lies in embracing
and celebrating people for who they are'
Richard Branson, Founder, Virgin Group

'There is no finish line when it comes to creating a more equal,
fair and just world. *How to Get Your Act Together* is a pivotal guide
for going from awareness to action in creating a more
diverse and inclusive workplace and society'
Marc Benioff, Chair and CEO, Salesforce

'The magic of diversity is that it protects us from our blind spots
and drives innovation – it makes all of us stronger. This book offers
ways to help you embrace what people can do and how they think,
rather than where they were born and what they look like'
Ajay Banga, Executive Chair, Mastercard

'Successful businesses rise on the shoulders of talented
employees who are confident bringing their authentic selves
to work. This book is a valuable guide for enabling leaders
to take action to ensure they can'
Beth Ford, President and CEO, Land O'Lakes, Inc.

'Diversity and inclusion are the gateways to stronger teams and better
performance. Fact. But it takes a good deal of self-awareness and
continuous learning to really ingrain the behavioural changes that are
needed. This book holds up a mirror and then guides us – skilfully
and persuasively – to the actions we all need to be taking'
Alan Jope, CEO, Unilever

ABOUT THE AUTHORS

Felicity Hassan is President of Audeliss, Inc., the US arm of Audeliss Ltd, a consultancy firm that levels the playing field for diverse executives and board members. Felicity serves on the board of the Women's Business Collaborative, where she also co-chairs the Advisory Council.

Suki Sandhu OBE is the Founder and CEO of Audeliss and INvolve, two globally recognized consultancy firms that champion diversity and inclusion in business. He is a Patron for akt, Board Director of OutRight Action International in New York and leads a fund via GiveOut to financially support LGBT+ activists in Asia.

HOW TO GET YOUR ACT TOGETHER

A Judgement-free Guide to Diversity and
Inclusion for Straight White Men

FELICITY HASSAN AND SUKI SANDHU

BUSINESS

PENGUIN BUSINESS

UK | USA | Canada | Ireland | Australia
India | New Zealand | South Africa

Penguin Business is part of the Penguin Random House group of companies
whose addresses can be found at global.penguinrandomhouse.com.

First published 2021
001

Copyright © Felicity Hassan and Suki Sandhu, 2021

The moral right of the copyright holders has been asserted

Set in 12/18pt Noah Grotesque
Typeset by Jouve (UK), Milton Keynes
Printed and bound in Great Britain by Clays Ltd, Elcograf S.p.A.

The authorized representative in the EEA is Penguin Random House Ireland,
Morrison Chambers, 32 Nassau Street, Dublin D02 YH68

A CIP catalogue record for this book is available from the British Library

ISBN: 978-0-241-48521-7

Follow us on LinkedIn: https://www.linkedin.com/company/penguin-connect/

www.greenpenguin.co.uk

This is for our husbands, our better halves,
our accomplices in love and life

CONTENTS

PREFACE

WHY DID WE WRITE THIS BOOK?

Felicity Hassan

There have been so many eye-opening moments that made me pause and think about the need to stand up and make a difference. I started working at fourteen and the instances of inappropriate behavior I experienced as a teenager are too numerous to mention. Post-university, I expected my transition into a corporate role to be night and day . . . I was going to be disappointed.

The more sexually oriented experiences of my earlier working years continued, from requests by senior leaders to go on dates to actual comments about my sexual performance and preferences. While these could have appeared career limiting, I had a fantastic manager who forewarned me how best to acknowledge, laugh and move on. This seemed admirable at the time, but now feels irresponsible, given those that may have felt less empowered to decline such advances.

I am grateful for the bravery of those who brought the #MeToo and #Black Lives Matter conversations to light. It will be incumbent upon all of us to ensure that we maintain this momentum and demand positive change.

My first salary negotiation really offered a turning point for me. Never having shied away from a tough conversation, I went boldly into an early career discussion with my MD, armed with data around what I'd achieved for the company, what I was yet to offer and what my value should be to my manager. The response, without hesitation and without any thought given to the preparation I'd clearly invested in the meeting, was, 'You are paid extremely well for a woman of your age.' Since age and gender evidently had zero bearing on the discussion, it was clear to me that something needed to be done.

My eyes were opened to the power of diversity in a corporate setting during my time at Bloomberg. I applaud Mike Bloomberg, for his unique stance on community and giving back, Peter Grauer, for the commitment he showed to holding the entire organization accountable for change, and Erika Irish Brown, for putting an early framework in place to make that change happen. This was my first exposure to the importance of straight white men and the power that their Allyship brings.

Their example, along with that of my own family, truly opened my mind to the importance of speaking up and being part of the solution. I consider myself extremely fortunate in the privilege that my parents afforded me through my education and upbringing. I have faced my fair share of challenges, but they pale by comparison to others'. With that in mind, I wanted to write this book with Suki. I have a responsibility to my family, my husband, our children and the next generation as a whole – to ensure that we unlock the immense power of Allyship in the fight for diversity, equity and inclusion for all.

Suki Sandhu

I remember the very start of my career and how I hated the Graduate Program I was undertaking. The company was hyper-masculine and I didn't feel like I fitted in. Then, seeing potential in my abilities, one of the managers took me under his wing and mentored me. He was my complete opposite. Straight, white, South African. He was what I now know to be an Ally. As a result of his taking an interest in me and supporting me, I became the company's best-performing consultant out of thousands of people globally. I wouldn't be where I am right now if Brad Shotland hadn't helped me launch the career journey I've been on. This includes founding two successful businesses in the diversity and inclusion space, earning an OBE from the Queen for the work I do, and helping countless candidates make career transitions and clients with their inclusion challenges. In 2016, having reflected on Brad's profound impact on my career, I personally thanked him. Here's the actual message, along with his reply:

Hi Brad – Just a quick note to say thank you for taking me under your wing when I was at Michael Page and close to quitting because I didn't like the environment and the job. I wouldn't be doing what I am now if you hadn't encouraged me to stay and learn.

Hi Suki – That is one of the nicest messages I have ever received. You are most welcome, but I saw something in you and I wasn't going to let that walk out the building. You are a very talented recruiter, as well as having grown into a phenomenal human being, and when you get your knight-hood, I will be first in line to congratulate you. Congratulations on all that you have achieved and I am proud to call you my friend (well, argumentative little shit at the time!!!) hahaha. Cheers, Brad

Can you imagine what millions of Allies could do for other people in business? That's why Felicity and I wrote this book. Everyone deserves to belong and you're the key to helping us unlock the inclusion we need. At INvolve, the global consultancy I founded to champion diversity and inclusion in business, we have a cross-company mentoring program. I've heard the feedback first-hand from mentees and mentors about the enriching experience it's given them. Not just the opportunities it's created for the mentees, from building their confidence to helping them navigate career challenges; but also the learning for the mentors about the lived experience of someone different to them in the workplace. It works. It does bring more inclusion. But I want you to be more than a mentor. I want you to act as a sponsor and be an Accomplice for diversity and inclusion. This book will show you how.

I personally tick many boxes: Indian, Sikh, gay, working class, married to a white, Catholic, German man. In work and in life, I have had numerous experiences of racism and homophobia. With seven nieces and nephews all under the age of eight, I want them to enter the workplace knowing they have the same opportunities as their white and male colleagues. With the current pace of change, equity will not happen in their lifetime. We have to act now and we need your help.

Having been in the world of diversity and inclusion for over fifteen years, I've seen the challenges companies face day in day out. I think straight white men are part of the solution. In fact, most straight white men want to be part of the solution, but they just don't know how and what action they're supposed to take. This book rectifies that with practical actions you can implement today.

So thank you for buying our book and joining us on this journey to get your act together.

INTRODUCTION

NUMBERS, STATISTICS, REALITY

Companies with over 30% women executives are more likely to outperform other companies,[1] yet:

- Men are 47% more likely to reach leadership positions than their female peers.[2]

- In the Russell 3000 Index, a benchmark of the entire US stock market, only 26% of the 307 US companies named women as CEOs.[3]

- Men make up 48.9% of the population of the US, with women at 51.1%, yet only 7.3% of Fortune 500 CEOs are women and only 1% are women of color.[4]

- 37% of UK FTSE companies have no ethnic representation in the boardroom. Yet tackling the racial disparities in the UK labor market could result in an annual economic boost worth £24 billion to the UK economy.[5]

US companies with an ethnically diverse leadership team outperform others by 36%[6] in the 2020 census and nearly 4 in 10 US residents identify as non-white, yet:

- There are only four Black CEOs in the Fortune 500[7] and 70% of senior leaders of color say their background has been a significant barrier.[8]

- Representation of ethnic minorities on US and UK executive teams stood at only 13% in 2019.[9]

- In the UK Race at Work Survey by Business in the Community, only 38% of employees feel that their employers are comfortable talking about race.[10]

YOU

Those statistics make for stark reading, yet they tell only half of the story around diversity and inclusion.

According to a 2018 report by the Human Rights Campaign Foundation, 46% of LGBT+ Americans remain closeted in the workplace.[11] The US Bureau of Labor Statistics reported in 2019 that only 19.3% of people with a disability were employed in the workforce.[12]

When Deloitte released its 2018 Millennial Survey report, it was clear that both Millennials and Generation Z believed that diversity is key to workplace loyalty – 69% said they were more likely to stay five years or more, if they perceived their employers to have a diverse workforce.

You may have seen some of these stats before. How do they make you feel? Frustrated? Scared? Surprised? Guilty? That's OK, and we are not here to judge you for this. Getting familiar with the state of affairs is the first and one of the biggest steps to creating real change. We want you to act now to make the positive changes in the right direction.

If you're a straight white guy who wants to:

• stay relevant

• see better working relationships in your organization

• create an equitable playing field for all

• progress in your career in a more competitive landscape

• be on the frontlines of creating a sea change in innovation and productivity for business across the globe

then this book is full of practical solutions for you.

Throughout our book, we will reference 'diversity and inclusion' a lot. D&I is the most common abbreviation for the term. However, you may hear 'diversity, equity and inclusion', or other elements like 'belonging' and 'impact'. For ease, we have tried to stick with D&I.

If you are ready and willing to embrace diversity and inclusion, but lack the know-how, this book is your new workplace companion.

If you're brave enough to be vulnerable, as a straight white male in a diverse workplace that demands success, this book will nurture your courage, strength and determination to succeed. D&I should work for everyone and this includes you.

The statistics reflect a workplace full of increasing complexity. So it's good to know there's a way forward for you to meet your targets and be effective at work, while learning to lead the way on diversity and inclusion.

If you want to harness the business case, here it is in these pages. If you're looking to push the boundaries and really make a difference, there's plenty of room here for you to work in.

But take note. If you want to be part of the solution as a leader in your organization, there's work ahead for you to do. All the way from awareness to action to becoming an Ally and Accomplice for the power of diversity and inclusion.

US

We are two people who have championed diversity and inclusion in business for almost forty years combined, and have been recognized for it by the Queen herself, so we like to think we have a few sensible ideas up our sleeves.

Suki founded Audeliss and INvolve, which tackle representation in leadership teams and boardrooms and help to build inclusive workplace cultures, respectively. Felicity leads the US arm of these businesses. We started our careers together over eighteen years ago and are the best of friends (most of the time!).

Working with people at senior levels in business, we both know full well that such change and much of the work in any organization fall to teams run by mid-level managers. That is, employees who have to take direction from above and implement strategies, policies and programs. So we wanted to produce a guide to help those employees. We often refer to leaders and managers in the book, but the content is equally valuable for individual contributors who are eager to learn more.

As a straight white man in a new world, you may be struggling with how to deliver diversity and inclusion because you do not consider yourself to be diverse. But you are the majority, especially at the top. Fact. We know that, if we don't encourage the majority to take action on diversity and inclusion, then the pace of change will be incredibly slow. We hope this book will give you the tools you need to accelerate positive change in your organization.

'Why should I care?' you might ask. If you join us on this journey, your company will be more creative, productive, innovative and profitable. Meaning, in turn, you'll be more fulfilled and satisfied in your role, as these benefits also apply to you, not just diverse communities. That's the business case in its simplest terms. Let's not also forget it's the right thing to do to care for your colleagues and ensure that everyone belongs. You've bought this book, so you must want to be part of the solution and we want to help you get there.

OUR ADVOCATES AND ALLIES

Throughout the book, you'll come across inspiring personal stories from very successful and high-profile white male leaders about their engagement with diversity and inclusion. We have had the privilege and opportunity to work with hundreds of leaders who have had incredible journeys as champions of inclusion. Their lessons and advice form an integral facet of the knowledge we want to share with you . . . just like this contribution from Jim.

JIM FITTERLING, CEO, DOW

I grew up in a small town in Missouri at a time when rural America wasn't very diverse. What it lacked in diversity, though, it made up for in life lessons, many of which I've applied throughout my career. One of the greatest lessons – one I learned from my dad – was about building teams and the uplifting power of diversity . . .

My dad was our high-school basketball coach. And I remember how he made sure all players were welcome on his teams – including Black players. In 1970s rural Missouri, that took a lot of courage. He stood up to angry fathers who thought their sons were losing playing time. We had eggs thrown at our house and cars. He faced a lot of hostility. But he stayed firm. He ensured the team – regardless of race – was made up of people who made them the most competitive. And they were good. They competed successfully all over the state against top teams because he put the best people on his team. It wasn't the easiest thing for him to do – but it was the right thing.

Like my dad, one of the jobs I have is making sure we have the best people on our team. And that means making sure everyone has an equal opportunity. A Black person who hasn't yet had the same opportunities as their white neighbor . . . someone with a physical disability or mental health challenge . . . a military veteran just back from serving their country . . . and a closeted gay kid from rural Missouri who never believed he could be a

CEO one day. All of those people have something in common: the ability to make a team better.

They offer a host of diversity – racial, cultural and neurodiversity, meaning they think differently. These differences – when we combine them in a team setting – provide new ways to compete and new ways to innovate and solve problems.

I try to keep that simple lesson my dad taught me in mind – and enable it through the organization – because we need all the diversity and all the problem solving we can get these days.

Dow is an American commodity chemical company listed on the New York Stock Exchange and has 54,000 employees across 160 countries and revenues of over $42 billion.

THIS BOOK

Planning this book, we asked several straight white men in our network what they felt when we raised the topic of their role in a diverse workplace.

Responses ranged from guilt to judgement, confusion and often a general fatigue.

Were we surprised? Not at all.

You're constantly bashed over the head with the concept of diversity with very little guidance on specifically what YOU can do to help. With so many resources out there, it can be incredibly challenging knowing where to start, so we've brought a lot of these resources together here. This is why we knew we had to create this book.

Have you ever felt like you couldn't say something you really wanted to at work? Have you ever felt like you had to hide something from someone for fear of how they'd react, or what they'd think of you? Have you ever felt like you're just 'faking it' all and someone's going to find you out? Have you ever felt like you aren't educated enough, lack the right skills, don't have the right personality or background to succeed?

We've all felt this way at some point. We've all felt like we aren't enough, or that we have to hide something, or that we aren't quite measuring up to expectations.

But has your *race* ever been the source of this feeling? Has your *sexuality* ever lost you a friend or a family member? Has your *gender* ever led people to question your ability?

We all face many barriers in the workplace, often due to factors outside of our control. The 'endgame' of diversity and inclusion is not to rebalance the scales more in favor of 'diverse' people to the detriment of straight white men. Instead, it's to make sure the fundamental aspects of anyone's identity are not the source of those barriers. As we've seen from the statistics already cited, this is sadly still the case for many. Indeed, straight white men who may be differently abled, neurodiverse or from a disadvantaged social background may face similar challenges. D&I seeks to remove those factors outside of our control and influence from inhibiting us on our path to success and progress. D&I is for everyone.

We want a better, more inclusive world. The last thing we want is for our straight white male readers to carry a burden of guilt or confusion through their lives, as they attempt to incorporate more diversity into their working environments and lives generally. Even as D&I professionals and from diverse communities ourselves, we have felt that confusion and guilt and it's not always productive. Part of the journey we'll take you on is to turn the ambiguity around D&I into some solid action and understanding.

As we show throughout the book, the nuances of language are key to breakthroughs in appreciating the importance of diversity and inclusion. We believe that progress in this area will be much easier when such discussions are commonplace at work. First, you need to understand the terminology, so we'll be taking a good look at that.

To help you in your work, we have divided the book into ten chapters.

Chapter 1 provides a foundation and asks you to explore and embrace **the opportunity of diversity**, as there'll be no progress without this.

Chapter 2 challenges you to choose **conscious inclusion**, by recognizing unconscious bias in everyone.

Chapter 3 gets you talking about **race** and understanding and combating microaggressions.

In **Chapter 4**, you'll learn how to listen to what **women** want and work for gender equity.

Chapter 5 will encourage you to find the language to really get to know and include your **LGBT+** colleagues.

Chapter 6 introduces ways to help you build bridges across **five generations in the workplace**.

In **Chapter 7**, we reinforce the message of **100% inclusion** for mental health and wellbeing, embracing disability, neurodiversity and social mobility.

Up to this point, each chapter presents **the case for diversity and inclusion** through its particular subject. Here, you'll find statistics, data, case studies and affirmations from business leaders who've done it and seen the benefits. Pointers to further research and practical exercises encourage you to turn theory into practice with your team.

Finally, each chapter prompts you to **take action with guidance on changes you can make immediately**.

The three remaining chapters – **8, 9 and 10** – take a different approach. In these, we focus on practical issues involved in implementing and delivering diversity and inclusion in the workplace.

Chapter 8 takes diversity for everyone into account through the increasing reality of **remote inclusion**. How do we keep inclusive when we're in different locations, even working from home?

Chapter 9 inspires you to **start recruiting inclusively** and takes you through some solutions you can implement.

Chapter 10 calls you to action as not only a straight white male Ally, but to **become an active Accomplice for diversity and inclusion in the workplace**.

We hope you accept this guidance around diversity and inclusion in the spirit we intend it. The world is changing fast and business leaders and social activists alike are spearheading this change. Thank you for being part of the solution and now let us help you get your act together!

CHAPTER 1

YOU ARE PART OF THE SOLUTION

In order to work towards a more inclusive culture, you first need to understand where the challenge begins. Multiple studies show that our bias towards those that look like us emerges at an extremely young age. Gender stereotypes can be seen as early as two and a half years old. This is where it begins.

If you were born a white cisgender male, you were born with privilege. The statistics we lead with in the book demonstrate that. We do not presume that you have not faced a multitude of challenges throughout your life. Far from it, we all face hurdles. We also know that being a white male has historically given you greater access and opportunity than others. This is often referred to as 'privilege' (we explore this concept in more depth on page 26). From the outset, we're asking you to take this as it is defined and not as an inherent negative. We're saying, as a white person with that privilege, your life may be tough, too, but your race, your sexuality and your gender have not been the source of those hurdles. And, if you can understand that, maybe you can realize why other people's lives are harder than they need to be.

We reference the term 'cisgender' from this point forward, so let's pause to explore what this means.

CISGENDER

cis·gen·der
/sis'jendər/

adjective
of, relating to, or being a person whose gender identity corresponds with the sex the person had or was identified as having at birth.[1]

How does cisgender relate to transgender?
If you were assigned female at birth and identify as a woman, you're a cisgender woman.

If you were assigned female at birth and identify as a man, you're a transgender man. Cisgender means the opposite of transgender.

We know how difficult it can be to understand diversity and inclusion when you may not identify as diverse. We're not here to make you feel bad about that. This book will help you understand the challenges and provide practical steps in how you can be part of the solution.

Later in this chapter, Neilsen's CEO David Kenny describes how he first learned to understand his own privilege. Like him, there's no reason why, historically, you would have understood what it is like to experience your workplace as someone Black, or who sees themselves as gender neutral, or what it is like to be a woman.

Here's the good news. None of this need remain a problem. Instead, if you're interested in learning how to tackle this journey, it's an incredible opportunity.

As a leader, you're probably someone who can look at workplace issues with curiosity and a desire to see everyone working together fairly and freely towards a common goal.

The journey will be tough. But remember, diversity and inclusion is not a zero-sum game. Inclusion benefits everyone, including you.

So don't worry if you're currently asking yourself these kinds of questions:

Is there a problem with diversity and inclusion in our workplace?
How do I know?
Am I part of the problem?
What do I do about it?

Are you part of the problem? The short answer is yes. But this also means you are part of the solution. And, as someone with privilege, you have more power to change things than you think. There's plenty you can do, starting by learning the language of diversity and inclusion, then understanding how to make a business case for action, to senior management and your team.

SO WHERE DO WE BEGIN?

'One of the greatest discoveries a man makes,
one of his great surprises, is to find he can
do what he was afraid he couldn't do.'

HENRY FORD[2]

While we're not suggesting we can change your belief structure, we do ask you to keep an open mind, as we explore how changing behaviors can make an enormous difference to those around you. Diversity and inclusion is a complex topic. You'll be meeting a wide variety of terms and opinions. The terms will often feel alien or confusing in the beginning. It's natural to have some concerns. We're here to help you learn more about all the key terms and issues. If you can talk it, you can walk it.

The illustration below[3] demonstrates visually how diversity, inclusion and equity intersect to create a workplace where everyone belongs, and shows problems that emerge when things are unbalanced.

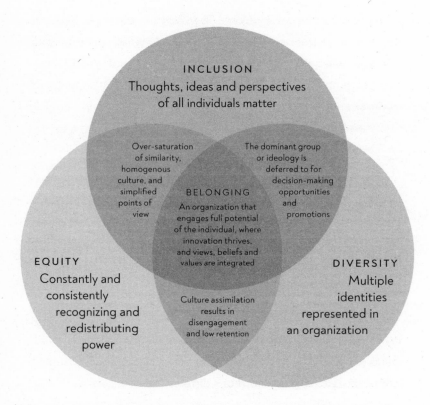

INCLUSION
Thoughts, ideas and perspectives
of all individuals matter

Over-saturation of similarity, homogenous culture, and simplified points of view

The dominant group or ideology is deferred to for decision-making opportunities and promotions

BELONGING
An organization that engages full potential of the individual, where innovation thrives, and views, beliefs and values are integrated

EQUITY
Constantly and consistently recognizing and redistributing power

Culture assimilation results in disengagement and low retention

DIVERSITY
Multiple identities represented in an organization

While you have heard them before and they may appear simple enough, these are big concepts that need better explanations. If belonging enables us to be our best and most productive self, then this is the diagram that holds the key:

Diversity

Diversity: the condition of having or being composed of differing elements.[4]

Diversity in an organization means a range of different identities, from race and gender to sexual orientation and ethnicity, religion, nationality, age, ability, disability and social background.

There's no such thing as a 'diverse person'. Groups and organizations can be diverse, but not individuals, although they may belong to a diverse community.

Malcolm Forbes summed it up pretty well: 'Diversity: the art of thinking independently together'.[5]

Inclusion

Although often used in tandem with diversity, inclusion is a concept of its own.

The Society for Human Resource Management defines inclusion separately from diversity as 'the achievement of a work environment in which all individuals are treated fairly and respectfully, have equal access to opportunities and resources, and can contribute fully to the organization's success'.[6]

Equity

Equality is ensuring that everyone has access to the same opportunities.

Equity ensures that everyone has the capability to access those same opportunities with freedom from bias or favoritism.

Equity recognizes that individuals start to access opportunities in an organization from different places, related to privilege, stereotypes and unconscious bias. Some need support to equalize their chance of accessing that opportunity.

While 'equity' is a term long used in the English language, it's often misunderstood due to its closeness to 'equality'. It can also be misapplied, due to its different meanings in different contexts, from justice to law, to finance and property. According to *Collins English Dictionary*, 'equity is the quality of being fair and reasonable in a way that gives equal treatment to everyone'.[7]

Whereas equality means ensuring that everyone has the same opportunities and receives the same treatment and support, equity is about giving more to those who need it, proportionate to their own circumstances, in order to ensure that everyone has the same opportunities. Equity aims to address the reality that not everyone can have the same opportunities unless they receive the support they need in the name of equality, giving them the same chance of getting there.

Although equality can be undermined where equity is not used effectively, the recognition of the importance of gender and racial equity in the workplace continues to grow.

EQUALITY

EQUITY

For example, do your hiring or promotion processes favor men? Consider a professional services firm like PwC. If you don't happen to have family members in that industry, you might not recognize the name. If you haven't gone to a select university where such organizations typically host recruiting drives, you might not even know the firm exists. This could mean that PwC is missing out on the talent in you. So what can the company do about that? Ensuring equitable access for such a firm would be engaging in community outreach and opening up alternative modes of entry, such as apprenticeships which don't require a degree and outreach which can be done with schools in disadvantaged areas. This is equity in action.

Everybody gets confused about equality and equity when they first come to grips with the difference.

If we think of equality as referring to equal opportunity and the same access to that for everyone in society, then it seems straightforward.

However, we need equity to go a step further, offering varying levels of support so that people who have restrictions of any kind can get to have that same access. For example, putting a ramp outside a building so that people in a wheelchair can get in and out just like able-bodied people.

Look at it this way and you can see that equality is literally treating everyone the same, as if there were no differences between people. But there clearly are so many differences. So when we get into equity, we're talking about fairness and 'equality in outcomes', as in the diagram on the previous page.[8]

In the simplest terms, we've added to Verna Myers's famous inclusion quote:[9]

Diversity is being invited to the party
Inclusion is being asked to dance
Equity is curating the playlist
Belonging is dancing like no one's watching.

LONGING FOR BELONGING

Belonging is about human inclusion, meaning 'everyone is included', no matter their identities, personalities and thinking styles. And yes, this includes you!

When we start with belonging, the rest should fall into place. If only the world were so simple. It isn't, so we have work to do on inclusion. Especially in a society built on meritocracy, a situation we're trying to change.

Unfortunately, while the concept of meritocracy often has noble intentions, we now know it to be a myth, often cited to justify not taking steps to be inclusive.

Michael Young coined the term 'meritocracy' in a tale called *The Rise of the Meritocracy 1870–2033*.[10] This satire was intended to inspire reflection upon the folly of meritocratic life – a system, organization or society in which people are chosen and moved into positions of success, power and influence on the basis of their demonstrated abilities and merit.[11]

While the aim of meritocracy was to reduce a system created around inherited status and offer equal opportunities for all, Young's satirical interpretation became mutated to suggest meritocracy as a positive construct, where people were awarded roles on merit rather than privilege.

From satirical roots to a convenient corporate interpretation, meritocracy in its current form certainly isn't having the desired impact of leveling the playing field and will either transform or cease to be used.

MORE DIVERSITY = GREATER PRODUCTIVITY, CREATIVITY, PROFITABILITY

Most business leaders need data and a clear business case to support the vision and plans they have for their organization and the people they employ.

Fortunately, there's a great deal of compelling and comprehensive research out there, showing that diverse business teams outperform non-diverse teams.

Isn't that great? The business makes more money, meaning that you hopefully earn more money too. Or, at the very least, you get greater job security yourself if the business is successful.

Our societies are becoming more diverse over time. With falling birth rates, we will need more support from immigrant labor to sustain our economies. The majority of Gen Z define themselves as something other than straight (52%),[12] so heteronormativity will no longer be the baseline assumption. Learning and adapting to all intersections of diversity are critical for your business to survive.

Before we get onto the business case, this is a good point to capture a useful bit of terminology in a word box. Look out for these. They appear in the first six chapters.

INTERSECTIONALITY

THE TERM: identifying how interlocking systems of power affect those who are most marginalized in society.

WHAT IT IS: a qualitative analytic framework from a branch of feminism, also called 'intersectional feminism', first coined in 1989 by Black feminist scholar Kimberlé Williams Crenshaw.[13]

CORE IDEA: discrimination on all aspects of social and political identity overlaps and intersects, e.g. race with gender, in the case of a Black woman who faces a double hurdle of discrimination, i.e. being Black and a woman.

AIMS: to acknowledge that we all have different experiences and identities.

WHERE IT'S GOING: now a broad-based term more about inclusion, referencing multiple demographics of diversity – disability, social mobility, mental health etc. More on this in Chapter 7.

Why not trust the business case for D&I and use it to your advantage?

Accenture's 2018 Getting to Equal research in South Africa shows that creating a culture of equality unlocks women's potential and allows everyone in the organization to thrive.[14]

Knowing the importance of diversity and inclusion is not the same as making it happen. Later in this chapter, David Kenny tells us he wants his hiring managers to take more chances. Following chapters will help you with the practicalities of bringing your vision to life. Look out for tips on recruiting inclusively in Chapter 9.

The research is sound. When McKinsey tells you that the business case for diversity and inclusion is becoming stronger than ever, you're going to sit up and listen, aren't you?[15]

While McKinsey's most recent analysis claims slow progress in gender and ethnic diversity in corporate leadership, it still shows that businesses in the top quartile for gender diversity are becoming increasingly likely to be more profitable than those with lower gender diversity.

2014	15% more likely
2017	21% more likely
2019	25% more likely
2025	?%*
* That's up to us.	

Or, as McKinsey puts it: 'the greater the representation, the higher the likelihood of outperformance'. They also use the kind of language most of us can relate to: 'the widening gap between winners and laggards'. Which group would you like your company to belong to? Hopefully, one that takes positive action and one that is winning.

PAY EQUITY AT SALESFORCE

Having made equity a core value of the company, Salesforce set about a full analysis of the salaries of 17,000 global executives to determine if men and women were paid equally for comparable work. It discovered that 6% of employees needed a salary adjustment, with approximately the same number of men as women affected. The company has spent $16 million since 2015 to eliminate statistically significant differences in pay.[16]

This has also led to it improving employee engagement and being one of Fortune's best companies to work for, helping it to attract more diverse talent.

REFORM AT REDDIT

Although Reddit is a top 20 global website, it has had a reputation as a platform for racist and misogynistic hate speech.[17] In recognition of this, venture capitalist and co-founder of Reddit, Alexis Ohanian, stepped down from the company's board to give his seat to a Black professional. He promised to use future gains from his Reddit stock to benefit the Black community, starting with a $1 million pledge to Know Your Rights Camp, an organization devoted to advancing the liberation and wellbeing of Black and brown communities.[18]

Let's not be complacent about this. The equivalent McKinsey figures for ethnic diversity show that progress here has stagnated. And the poor diversity performance of the 'laggards' has actually declined further over the last half a decade.

What makes a difference for the winners? McKinsey is clear on that. Two critical factors: a systematic business-led approach to D&I and bold action on inclusion, both supported by clear actions:

1. Increase diverse representation, particularly in leadership and critical roles

2. Strengthen leadership capabilities for D&I and accountability for delivering on D&I goals

3. Enable equality of opportunity through fairness and transparency

4. Promote openness, tackling bias and discrimination

5. Foster belonging through support for wide-ranging diversity.

While it's easy to make a list, you'll be glad to hear that this book will show how to action these points. In our troubled social and economic times, your business wants to make more money. Greater gender, ethnic and cultural diversity is a clear way to do that.

That said, this isn't just about financial results. Diversity and inclusion brings with it more creativity, improved productivity and higher engagement from your employees. Inclusive employers are businesses people are happy to work for, where they feel they belong and where they feel like they are an essential cog in the machinery that makes it all operate smoothly. All of this means employees feel more inspired and motivated to contribute and work harder towards the common goal of business success when they have a sense of being included.

WANT TO KNOW MORE?

Starting with the Introduction of this book, you're gathering together some useful stats to show you mean business.

You'll pick up plenty more as we go through.

Later in the book we've collected a whole raft of useful information, resources and links.

Go to Further Resources, page 236.

A CLOSER LOOK
AT PRIVILEGE

We've made the business case for greater diversity in the workplace as a means to get you financially motivated to be a part of the solution. But what about the social argument, the right for us all to belong? This goes far beyond financial performance.

Let's explore the concept of privilege in more depth. It's such a hot word. What's the first thing you think of when you read it? How does it make you feel? What do you think it means? The word produces myriad reactions in everyone. And that's normal, nothing to feel guilty about, but this makes it an uncomfortable subject for many, nonetheless.

A lot of those who have privilege either don't want to or don't know how to talk about it. Those who don't appear to have it may assume that others do and are eager to avoid the topic. As a result, there's not much conversation happening at all.

So how about first understanding your own sense of privilege?

> **PRIVILEGE**
>
> priv·i·lege
> /ˈpriv(ə)lij/
>
> *noun*
> a special right,
> advantage or
> immunity granted
> or available only
> to a particular
> person or group.[19]
>
> *'education is a
> right, not a
> privilege'*

Three Things You May Not Have Considered If You Identify as a Straight White Man

- If a traffic cop pulls you over, you can be sure it's not down to your racial profile

- You probably don't think twice about walking out late at night alone

- You're not likely to anger anyone about the toilet you use

'Privilege' is not a dirty word, but these examples are how privilege works. In many parts of the world today, if you have white skin, you're privileged in many ways, despite being an overall minority among 7 billion people.

Shocked? Don't be. Privilege is everywhere. It is relative to those around you, your community and your culture. It is also contextual. For instance, if you were born in the country you live in, you have privileges in terms of access to rights and benefits no immigrants will possess even if they speak the native language. In the UK, where access to National Health Service healthcare is available and free at point of need to all comers, new research from Doctors of the World shows that migrants in England are being denied care for an average of thirty-seven weeks.[20]

A good example of white privilege in the US is shown in the fallout from 'redlining', a system once used by banks and the real estate industry that literally outlined in red ink the neighborhoods where people of color lived. If you lived inside the red lines, you were considered risky and banks were less likely to give loans or invest. The practice was banned in 1968, but the impact lives on, historically preventing Black families from amassing wealth at the same rate as their white neighbors on the other side of that red line. This had a trickle-down effect on education, with far-reaching implications. We explore race inclusion in more depth in Chapter 3.

Being born into a well-off family can give you privilege in terms of the education, health and leisure activities you take part in as a child. That isn't your fault, but it is a privilege to be aware of. If you are an able-bodied person, the way you plan and live your life will be different from someone with a physical or emotional disability.

It's all privilege.

Q&A

Q: But we live in a meritocracy, don't we? If you're good enough, you'll get the job.

A: That's what we like to think, yes, but bias and historical context still influence us greatly – we haven't reached meritocracy yet.

Capture your initial reaction. Be honest with yourself. How does this make you feel?

Mixed thoughts? Not yet ready to accept it? Where's the evidence?

While there's plenty of evidence in this book, we've no intention of leaving you high and dry at this point in the journey. Perhaps it's time to understand where and how privilege exists in your workplace. Most of the chapters in this book contain a practical exercise for you and your team to work through one of the hot topics of diversity and inclusion. No better place to start than privilege.

Some examples of privilege

Privilege extends over many aspects of life: your gender, the color of your skin, your socio-economic position, your spiritual association, your sexual orientation. Pretty much everything, then . . .

Gender Privilege

If you're a man, do you even notice the privileges you're accorded on the basis of your gender? How about swapping pay with your female colleagues at the same level for, say, five years? What would it feel like if people deferred only to women in the room and left you out?

White Privilege

Do you live in a country where white privilege benefits white people at the expense of people of color? Any idea what it's like to be typecast for the color of your skin, or to have to search high and low for products that suit your skin? What do you think it would feel like if the culture you live in did not cater for you?

Socio-economic Privilege

What is it that you need, but can't afford? How would it feel to know that you could smash that educational course if only you had the resources to take it? What about choosing between paying for the healthcare of your child or food on their plate?

Religious Privilege

Have you ever had to worry about finding an appropriate place of worship near you? Can you imagine not feeling a sense of connection between your religious celebrations and wider society? What if you couldn't get a day off from work for your religious holidays?

Heterosexual Privilege

Remember when you were fifteen and had to come out as a straight white heterosexual male? No, because society accepted you just as you were. So try to imagine feeling scared to hold hands with your significant other in public, or not being able to take that person home to meet your family for the holidays?

GET DOWN TO IT

Our perspectives are formed by our experiences as individuals and as part of social groups. This exercise could help you lead a discussion within your team about how experiences of race, ethnicity, gender, sexual orientation, ability, socio-economic status or religious identity affect the way individuals experience the world. But first you've got to get there yourself.

Circles of Influence Exercise

You're going to take a sheet of paper and list different types of people in your life.

Simply write down the name of the first person who comes to mind for each.

Do this BEFORE reading the debrief notes at the end.

Here are some suggested prompts:

your best friend
your room-mate (or hallmate)
your favorite professor
your favorite actor or actress
your favorite fictional character
the author of the last book you read for pleasure
a religious or spiritual leader
a famous leader you admire
your doctor
your hair stylist

Debrief
Finally, against the list, add the race, gender and sexual orientation that each individual name would identify with.

Are you surprised by the patterns you saw in your own list? Why?

You may feel uncomfortable if most of the people you named are within the same racial category. The objective is not to shame participants for their selections, but rather to help them reflect upon who resides in their spheres of influence and appreciate how that forms the basis of both their privilege and their bias.

Now, as we reach the end of this foundation chapter on how you can be part of the solution, how about taking a couple of minutes to absorb how this was all put into practice by business leader David Kenny, who accepted that Nielsen had a systemic bias in their workplace, and so began to identify opportunities to break it down.

A LEADER OPENS UP
ABOUT HIS WHITE PRIVILEGE

DAVID KENNY, CEO, NIELSEN

Early in my career, I had a Black female colleague on my team, and someone assumed she was on the cleaning staff. She told me that it happened often, and I saw through her eyes, at that moment, how people were making assumptions based on her skin color and gender.

As a white male, you don't have to prove yourself. There aren't any negative assumptions – people believe you have a level of competency that opens up opportunities in education, at work, and within your network. That's why, over time, I've worked hard to make sure that I'm sensitive to those assumptions – my own and those I'm with – and treating all people with dignity and respect.

As CEO, I know that I have even more privilege. When I'm in meetings, I make sure that I'm facilitating the conversation instead of being the talker all the time. I invite others to speak up, and redirect any negative assumptions or comments. After a meeting, I try to be a good mentor and provide feedback to encourage the more reticent ones to speak up more in future.

White people with privilege must be willing to give up some of that privilege, starting with opening up opportunities. I personally support Teach for America and Year-Up because it's important to create a path for young people starting in the classroom and then with their first job. We need more great teachers who believe in their students regardless of their background or skin color. We need more hiring managers who are willing to take a chance and give you that first job. The reality is that we have not eliminated racism or sexism and the first step is to help people recognize their own biases.

Nielsen is a leading global data and analytics company that provides a holistic and objective understanding of the media industry. With 14,000 employees, Nielsen offers measurement and analytics services in nearly 60 countries.

ARE YOU FEELING MORE CONFIDENT?

There's a way to go for diversity and inclusion in the workplace – all the way to 100% inclusion.

It's a task that belongs to society. Cultural change takes time. But you can be part of the solution in your organization, starting now.

If we're doing our job properly, you're hopefully beginning to understand that, in terms of diversity and inclusion, being a white male leader is not a problem for you, but an opportunity. Everyone benefits from diversity and inclusion, including straight white men.

If you're feeling the pressure, that's a sign your curiosity is taking you places you've never been before. It means you've accepted the reality that ignoring or avoiding diversity and inclusion is no longer an option for anyone at work or in the wider world.

If we have to conclude with anything here, it's David Kenny's advice: question your assumptions, open up some opportunities, take a few chances. Trust yourself.

WHAT ARE YOU WAITING FOR?

By taking this first huge step of admitting the problem, you are already beginning to create the opportunity for change in your workplace.

GET YOUR ACT TOGETHER

Recognize that, as a straight white male, you are part of the solution.

There is a business case for inclusion – accept it exists and is valid.

Remember that inclusion benefits everyone, including you.

Equality is key, but it's equity that makes it happen.

Undertake the exercise in this chapter, understand your privilege and use it for good.

NEXT>>>>>   PUT BIAS IN ITS PLACE

CHAPTER 2

PUT BIAS IN ITS PLACE

Take yourself through a short visual imagination exercise, which we've adapted from Valerie Alexander.[1] Then, if it works, try it with your team:

• Close your eyes and imagine you are at the airport. You're late for a flight, you're rushing to the gate and just make it in time . . .

• You're stepping inside the plane with the door shutting behind you and the pilot has popped out of the cockpit and says hello.

• You get to your destination and go to a local restaurant and you have the most delicious meal. Next to you, you see a couple celebrating a special anniversary meal.

• The next morning, you go to the biggest technology conference in the world and the CEO of this year's hottest tech start-up is just taking the stage to speak . . .

Hopefully, you should have a solid picture of those instances we've just described. Now we have some questions for you. We'd like you to picture your answers in your mind.

In your mental image, was the pilot Black? Was the married couple two men? Was the tech CEO who took the stage a woman?

It's OK if one or all of your answers is no. Your brain creates images of what is familiar. The images you saw – and your biases – are built from your socialization, the media, your experiences, and they are natural. We all have them.

It doesn't mean that you will always act on the automatic part of your mind. What really counts is what you do about your biases, and that you recognize when they might be cropping up. Which is why it is important that you question your decisions on a daily basis.

Key questions:

How can you move away from what your mind automatically assumes and reach a more inclusive place?

While these visualizations are just images, what assumptions are you making when you meet real people?

THANK GOODNESS FOR BIAS

Where would we be without our ability to tell the difference between one thing and another? Chalk and cheese? Wheat and chaff? Truth and BS?

Coming down on the side of something we favor serves us very well as human beings. We make our choices and they often define who we are. Our football team, our favorite food, the movies we recommend. We stand by them, with some passion. Bias has been an important factor in our survival as a species since the beginning of time, helping us make the quick decisions we need to overcome threats and thrive.

But what happens when we use our bias to discriminate against someone without even realizing we're doing it? Black and white. Straight and gay. Woman and man. Young and old.

Here are some quick examples:

As a teenager, Nathan went off the rails. Hardly surprising, he came from a very poor area. But Simone went to private school and had everything, so she has no reason to fail now.

Although there was nothing to separate the two candidates, Parmjit had to make a decision. He chose Mia, as she was extrovert and talkative, just like him.

We all do this. Or something like this. The people around us in our workplace have a range of different biases. We have biases. Everyone demonstrates a bias against someone, somewhere, sometime.

Bias also gets into our policies and stays there for years. We only hire graduates for these positions? Why? Later in the chapter, you'll see CEO Greg Case talking about how this happened at Aon and what the company did to counter this bias when they recognized it for what it was.

Unsurprisingly, we're shy about our own biases. Who wants to admit to what others might consider a weakness? Or worse, a prejudice? This may well be why we hear people saying that unconscious-bias training doesn't work.

Admittedly, unconscious-bias training (in its traditional form) does not work. It tends to just reveal why we have biases and stops there. Without any follow-up, or action planning, unconscious-bias training makes it seem like, well, it's unconscious, so I can't do anything about it. End of story. Our biases won't go away easily, some not at all and some only with lots and lots of time and practice.

We once had bias explained to us as being like an addict in recovery – you never stop having the potential to fall into your old traps, so you're constantly taking steps and reflecting to ensure you don't go there again. This is why in INvolve we transform unconscious bias into conscious inclusion – there has to be a conscious effort to fight, question and examine bias, every day. You completed a conscious-inclusion exercise at the start of this chapter.

For now, what are the most common biases you'll meet in the workplace? This isn't a joke or a trick question.

The answer is a model coined ACE.[2] We often think of bias in terms of the *people* it affects – through gender, ethnicity, disability and more. While we apply ACE to people, it actually stands for the unconscious *attitudes* we hold around certain areas before we apply it to people. These areas specifically are:

A Ability, Ambition
Ability bias – college graduates were smarter to begin with, so they would have earned more money than the typical high-school graduate, even if they didn't go to college.

C Commitment, Connections
Commitment bias – feeling pressured to keep things consistent, even though it goes against what you truly want to do, your future goals and everything you've ever said about yourself.[3]

E Emotional Intelligence, Executive Presence
Executive Presence bias – someone who is more of an introvert is assumed to not be a 'leader'.

When we make decisions about people, we may describe what influences us as 'gut-level assumptions' or 'intuition'. Yet developing the potential of diversity in any team calls for a manager, and the team at large, to get beyond these biases. The ACE definitions are common bias areas for us all to be mindful of.

So let's not be tentative about this. There are times when you must take action on bias in the workplace. We understand you're going to want some ideas and techniques to deal with the issue as you come across it. You're going to need to call out bad behavior where you see it, when you see it. Then explain why that action displayed negative bias without being euphemistic, without softening the blow.

Acknowledging our own biases is the best place to start. How can we fight biases if we don't even recognize our own? Take courage. We've been there, and we're on your side.

BEGIN WITH YOUR BIAS

'I'm not biased,' we hear you say. That's lovely to hear, but we all have bias – Suki is biased towards diversity and knows he probably gives straight white men a tougher time in a recruitment process, so interviews in pairs to mitigate it. Felicity has a bias towards communication style and once thought all should assimilate to one approach. After lived experience and research, she understands that this is detrimental to those impacted and limits individual expression.

In trying to be helpful, observant, insightful or collaborative, we often mean well, little realizing that our words can have a negative impact.

Sometimes, one statement can contain several biases. The speaker thinks they are saying one thing, while revealing another.

What would happen in your workplace if you and your colleagues became more aware of your various biases? Your unconscious – and let's be honest, sometimes very conscious – attitudes and thoughts that sometimes cloud your judgement of other people? Could you become more aware of who they are as an individual and think about how to include them before you act?

It's time for a bit of useful jargon. Remember when Kanye West took the microphone off Taylor Swift during the 2009 MTV *Video Music Awards*?[4] They called that 'manterrupting', the unnecessary interruption of a woman by a man. Some people began talking about a 'No-Kanye' rule.

If you've ever heard of 'mansplaining' – that situation in meetings where a man explains to a woman how something works in a very condescending way, and often when she knows exactly what she's talking about in the first place – then 'hepeating' takes it a step further.

HEPEATING

THE TERM: hepeating, alternatively known as 'bropropriating', was first coined in 2017 by friends of astronomer and professor Nicole Gugliucci.[5]

WHAT IT MEANS: when a woman suggests an idea and it's ignored, but then a man says the same thing and everyone loves it.

CORE IDEA: consciously or unconsciously undermining and discrediting the intellectual property of women in the workplace.

AIMS: to raise awareness of this activity and use the term 'hepeating' to call it out.

WHERE IT'S GOING: women are not alone in being hepeated; it also happens to people of color and other marginalized communities.

These are all examples of a fairly common demonstration of bias, thinking we have something more important or valuable to say than someone else, and feeling the need to make sure our voice is heard or we have the last word. We've all done it. But for some groups, often women, this happens multiple times a day, hundreds of times a week, countless times over a lifetime. This creates a culture that rewards extroversion and assertiveness in men and inhibits or outwardly judges women for being the same. Sometimes it's not the isolated instance of one individual's bias that's the problem, but the fact that so many of us do it that conflates it into a larger problem.

YES, THERE'S EVEN A SCIENCE OF BIAS

There's a good chance you already know a great deal about bias, even if you aren't aware of the specific names for different types. And some of them you don't even know you have.

Look Out for These Biases in Your Workplace

Affinity bias	*Halo/Horns effect*
This bias refers to our tendency to gravitate towards people similar to ourselves.	**The tendency to put someone on a pedestal or think more highly of them after learning something impressive about them, or conversely, perceiving someone negatively after learning something unfavorable about them.**
Everybody in Judy's team went to Oxford University, except Jane. No point inviting Jane to the Thursday night pub quiz, as she just wouldn't get it.	I've never worked with anyone like Shonagh for diligence and creativity. But seeing her wearing face and body metal on dress-down Friday really detracts from her performance.
Benevolent bias	*Attribution bias*
This bias occurs when our efforts to be kind result in us making decisions on other people's behalf that take away their choices.	**This bias refers to the systematic errors made when people evaluate or try to find reasons for their own and others' behaviors.**
Jennifer has just come back from maternity leave, so she wouldn't want to go for a promotion just yet, given all the childcare issues she has right now.	Derek took five years to complete a four-year degree. He must have failed a year somewhere. It's the rejection pile for his CV.

MOVE FROM UNCONSCIOUS BIAS TO CONSCIOUS INCLUSION

While you can conduct training with your team on unconscious bias, it's worth addressing and understanding your own unconscious bias first. Yes, we keep repeating this. It's important.

You may find that you yourself are having to correct the behavior you've lived with all your life to date. In which case, you'll understand how your team may feel when you first introduce the concept.

Your task is to frame this first and foremost as a challenging but positive experience. It's going to be about the language you use. Why not call it a 'Conscious Inclusion Workshop'?

Simply changing the language to be more positive has an immediate effect which is not the 'eye roll'. True, some biases are unconscious, but many are also conscious efforts of our minds rationalizing and making decisions – mitigating bias is often just about taking a pause and thinking of something from a different angle. 'Unconscious' really makes it sound like we can't mitigate it when in fact we can. Unfortunately, there will always be cynics, but this is something you'll have to manage.

A useful path through is to make this real. When have you experienced bias? Or have you seen your friends or family experience bias? Have you been judged for your education? Accent? Clothes? How much money you have? Have you ever felt the need to cover for your religion, or caring for kids or family, because you wanted to avoid judgement? All of us can be on the sharp end of bias.

When Audeliss worked with Nationwide Building Society to help recruit a board member, this is how the chairman addressed bias.

POSITIVE ACTION

BOARDROOM DIVERSITY AT NATIONWIDE BUILDING SOCIETY

Leading what had historically been an entirely white board, David Roberts, the chairman of Nationwide Building Society, one of the UK's largest financial institutions, needed to recruit a new board member and so retained a search firm to find the widest talent pool possible. David was conscious that bias could potentially feature in the selection process based on the existing diversity profile of the board, so when they were down to two final candidates, including an Indian woman from outside of banking, action was taken to seek further opportunity, through referencing and interviews, for the Indian candidate to be able to demonstrate her ability to the full. The Indian candidate was appointed, and it was regarded as a positive intervention by the board to ensure an inclusive approach.

WANT TO KNOW MORE?

If you'd like to come to grips with your own unconscious bias, you can access several tests from Harvard, covering race, sexuality, weight and other areas.

Go to Further Resources, page 237.

Admitting to the existence of bias is one thing, tackling it effectively quite another. Next, Greg Case describes what he discovered in his organization and how Aon set about creating greater inclusion.

A LEADER TALKS ABOUT UNCONSCIOUS BIAS IN HIS OWN ORGANIZATION

GREG CASE, CEO, AON PLC

I grew up knowing that college wasn't a given, but that if I worked hard, I was likely to get there and that my future success was largely within my own control. Because, as a white male, success was exactly that – up to me. It was a formula of commitment, discipline and effort. But I've realized later in life that the formula is more complicated for some than others. That realization was reinforced when we launched our apprentice program at Aon, opening our doors to candidates without a college degree.

That's how I met Victor and Ed, two of the young men in our first apprentice class. Before they came to Aon, they were doing everything right – working hard and doing so with great drive and discipline. But minimum wage only gets you so far. And community college, the most affordable option, can generate opportunities for advancement, but doesn't typically create a corporate job track.

One young man was working two jobs – fast food and hospitality – going to school at night and raising a young family; the other was working nights in a warehouse and going to school during the day. But even with that drive and discipline, success wasn't just up to them, it was also up to us. Because what we have at this moment is not a failure of supply – the talent is out there doing everything right and striving to get ahead. It is a failure to create interest or demand that recognizes what these driven and committed colleagues can deliver, simply because they lack the typical connections or usual validators.

There are unconscious biases towards race and gender but also an underlying view that hard work is all it takes to get through the door. For those of us already at the table, it's a comfortable fiction.

We continue to expect work ethic, discipline and excellence in our colleagues at Aon, but we're also taking our apprentice program global, because those qualities exist outside of traditional talent pipelines and we're committed to creating more opportunities for diverse colleagues. Victor and Ed's success at Aon is a testament to that idea and a reminder that we need to keep the door open for others.

Aon is a NYSE-listed global professional services firm, with more than 50,000 colleagues, using proprietary data and analytics to provide a broad range of risk, retirement and health solutions to clients in 120 countries.

THERE IS SOMETHING YOU CAN DO ABOUT BIAS

If you can put in the time to provide your team with a well-run workshop and good follow-up conversations on an individual basis, you'll be amazed how much change you'll see in the way people communicate and behave.

Make training a positive experience for people and you'll soon notice them stepping out of their comfort zones and being prepared to experiment, even take risks, as you have yourself. Start off by explaining that everyone has biases, just different biases and there are many to have.

But training isn't the be all and end all. Training is a good place to start, but ensure follow-up conversations are happening, whether that's in one-on-ones or in performance review meetings. Your team members need to know that inclusion isn't just something you think about for an hour every year, but something that needs to be demonstrated across the team every day.

Yes, it's a serious subject, but if you create a safe space for discussion you can also have a bit of fun with some of the biases people don't even know they have. Just be sure to call out everyday bias in the workplace when you see and hear it – it's your responsibility as a leader.

How to Call Out Bias – Our 'Go To' Tips

- **Get people to reflect:** It's often unlikely that someone said or did something biased out of malice – ask probing questions to get them to see the error in their ways themselves, before calling them out more directly. 'What do you mean by that?' 'Do you really think that?' 'Did you mean to say it like that?' In some one-on-one instances, a prolonged silence and questioning look can be enough.

- **If you're unsure if it was discrimination/bias:** If you find that you were unable to act in the moment, it's never too late to say something. Take the person aside at a later date after you've reflected and seen that what was said/done was discrimination. Try to come at it from a standpoint of education, offering resources and information to help them learn why it was wrong.

- **If it's explicit and direct discrimination:** Call it out directly for what it is and do it in the moment. Stop it in its tracks and make clear that discrimination is not to be tolerated. Follow up with

anyone who might have been affected and make sure they are
OK. Ask what support they need and if there's anything they'd
like you to do. Independently, if you feel it warrants reporting,
report it.

• **Practice makes perfect:** Practice in a safe environment with family
or friends by role playing situations. Calling people out is hard,
but it gets easier the more you do it. The first time you do it, you
might fumble, and it will probably be awkward, but keep going.

GET YOUR ACT TOGETHER

Everyone is biased, it's part of human nature.

Our collective problem is unconscious bias, which exists
inside and outside the workplace.

When you see or hear bias, make sure you call it out and
call it what it is – don't be euphemistic in your language as
it undermines the person experiencing the bias.

As a leader, your best first step is to understand your own
bias, so take the online Harvard test (see Further
Resources: Bias, page 237).

Your responsibility is to make training a safe and positive
experience so try the conscious-inclusion exercise about
the airport with your colleagues.

NEXT>>>>>   LET'S TALK ABOUT RACE

CHAPTER 3

LET'S TALK ABOUT RACE

Welcome to the most difficult conversation in business: race. With Black Lives Matter, the media is full of it and it seems you're right in the middle of it. Yet the silence about racism in your workplace may be deafening.

Who is going to be bold enough to break that silence and get effective discussions about race up and running on a level that makes a real difference in the workplace? You? Well, yes, you're the person in the hot seat.

Naturally, you're going to have some questions . . .

How do I avoid getting tied in knots by people who know more about race than me?

Shouldn't people of color be leading any discussions about race?

If being white is the problem, how do I even begin?

What would be a meaningful and helpful discussion about race?

If the system is at fault, then how can I make a difference as just one person?

What are these microaggressions that I hear people whispering about?

It's possible you're feeling like the last person to be initiating and leading discussions around race in your workplace. You can already anticipate tension. You know that people will express strong opinions and some will get upset.

But don't worry, help is at hand. You're not the only leader in this position, so there's plenty of information available out there to help you start this well and keep it on track.

Later in the chapter, you'll read about how Salesforce CEO Marc Benioff championed a #BlackLivesMatter activist, and used the backlash to get a conversation going. While getting things wrong is inevitable in the journey, it shouldn't stop you from continuing towards your destination. Salesforce is not shy about taking action on Black inclusion in business. It has set a goal of increasing its Black representation by 50% by 2023, as well as doubling Black representation at VP level and above in the same time period. While developing policy and promoting philanthropic objectives are important, it's making this knowledge public that holds Salesforce accountable for taking action.

Since there isn't anybody, including yourself, who hasn't thought about the subject of race, it's best to start with the big 'Why?'

Remember, this is not a discussion around whether any single one of us dislikes the skin color of anybody else. You're not trying to identify and weed out racists. The aim is to foster inclusion and learn how everyone can play their part in dismantling the obstacles that prevent people of color gaining equal opportunities at work.

You, too, can be brave and encourage the dialogue for change to happen. You can begin by understanding the difference between race, ethnicity and nationality.[1]

RACE	Physical characteristics that define you as belonging to a specific group: *facial features, physical build, skin color, hair color and texture* *White or Caucasian* *Black or African American* *Asian* *American Indian or Alaska Native* *Native Hawaiian or Pacific Islander*
ETHNICITY	Cultural characteristics that define you as belonging to a specific group: *social customs, religion, language, accent, dress and hairstyles, dietary preferences* *Caribbean* *American* *Middle Eastern* *South American* *African* *European*
NATIONALITY	Legal definition identifying you as being a member of a specific nation state: *citizenship* *British* *American* *Chinese* *German* *Italian* *Kenyan*

So if someone refers to their race as 'Black', their ethnicity might be South American, or someone may say their race is 'white', and their ethnicity is Middle Eastern. For example, Suki's race is Indian, he would define his ethnicity as European and his nationality as British. Felicity is white, her ethnicity is European and American as she's lived for long lengths of time in both places, and her nationality is British. In its simplest terms, your race is what you're born with, your ethnicity is the culture you grew up in and nationality is the country on your passport.

What if we experiment with adding your race/ethnicity/nationality to your email signature below your pronouns and job title, which are other important parts of your identity? If someone is curious, then they know they can talk to you about it. It would look something like this:

Suki Sandhu OBE
Founder & CEO
[he/him/his]
[Indian/European/British]

Felicity Hassan
President US
[she/her]
[Caucasian/European & American/British]

This would of course be totally voluntary, but imagine how quickly we would begin to learn and understand more about people we work with, and how many more conversations about our identities, heritage, religions and other important topics we could have. And yes, this includes you talking about your background.

WHICH COMES FIRST – RACE, ETHNICITY OR NATIONALITY?

Getting to grips with the differences in these terms is one thing. But when you have real people in front of you, who are you dealing with?

It's all about context. Take ethnicity, for example. The only way for you to appreciate differences between, say, a Latinx and Hispanic person is to learn all about what makes those differences. Assumptions just won't do. If Latinx is defined as someone who hails from a South American background, it doesn't mean they speak Spanish, or even Portuguese. An indigenous language could be their first tongue. While we might expect a Hispanic to speak Spanish, it doesn't mean they're from South America. From the table opposite, a person's language defines their ethnicity only.

Now, what if that person is Black or Caucasian? Could they still be Hispanic or Latinx? Yes, because now we're talking about their race, not just their ethnicity. Taken together, ethnicity and race could present a Spanish-speaking Black person, leaving you guessing at their nationality. That's because ethnicity and race exist within the context of a national environment.

Let's picture a person from Spain who is Caucasian and who

LATINX

/laˈtiːnɛks,ləˈtiːnɛks/

noun
a person of Latin American origin or descent (used as a gender-neutral or non-binary alternative to Latino or Latina).

'the books share stories of the civil rights struggle for African Americans, Latinx and LGBTQ people'

adjective
relating to people of Latin American origin or descent (used as a gender-neutral or non-binary alternative to Latino or Latina).

'a unique Latinx perspective that other shows don't really capture'[2]

states her ethnicity as Basque. Yes, she can have more than one ethnicity. Her first choice may be Basque, and she may speak that indigenous language as well as Spanish, but she is a citizen of Spain. What happens when she moves to the United States or the UK? Her national context is altered. She may be treated as a Spaniard from Spain, or even a white European. She may personally identify as Basque, but, according to its customs and procedures, her new country will probably see her ethnicity more broadly – as Spanish or European.

This overview highlights the complexity of race, ethnicity and nationality and calls you to get to know the individual rather than making assumptions about their background or heritage. If it's appropriate, then you will probably learn this information as you get to know your colleagues better. What is more important is the rich diversity that brings different experiences and perspectives to the workplace which will help us innovate and unlock new opportunities.

Race and ethnicity are separate categories. A person's ethnicity often depends on both cultural and national contexts.

THE WORK IS STILL TO DO

Representation matters: in Fortune 500 companies, there are only three Black CEOs (0.6%) (December 2020).[3]

In the UK, at the time of the 2014 Parker Review recommending greater ethnic diversity in the boardroom, there were two Black CEOs in the top three positions of FTSE 100 companies. By 2020, that had reduced to zero. Only 10 out of 297 directors had ethnic-minority backgrounds, the same as in 2014.[4]

Imagine an Asian, Black or Hispanic graduate who sees an incredible amount of diversity at the lower levels of the business and no senior leaders who reflect their identity. They look up at the white snowy peaks of the organization chart and wonder, 'How on earth do I get there?'

Challenges of representation within an organization are intensified by everyday experiences of what we call 'microaggressions'. These often take the form of innocuous comments that may or may not seem harmful to the people making them. We should not give the false idea that microaggressions are innocent, when they're often a gateway that allows racism into the workplace, with little to no recourse for the victim.

Microaggressions that build up over time can often result in diverse talent leaving the business, making the representation challenge that much harder to solve.

Executives vs the rest of the labor force

While Hispanic Americans make up 17% of the workforce, they only make up 4% of company executives.

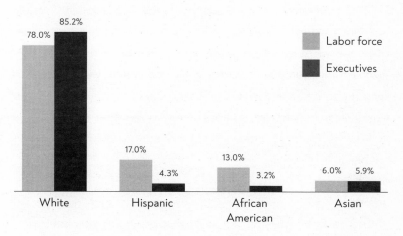

One example we often hear is 'Where do you come from?' Yet all we're doing is indicating to the person that we're asking due to their skin color and perhaps assuming they're not from here, that they don't belong and might never belong.

Go back to the race, ethnicity and nationality point we made earlier. Think about what you're really asking. Try putting yourself in their shoes. We all appreciate the need to get to know our peers but asking about heritage is not an icebreaker, it's something that you might explore once you have already built a relationship with that person. At that point, if you are still genuinely curious, then perhaps lead with some information about yourself and encourage your colleague to do the same: for instance 'I grew up in England before moving to New York for work. What about you?'

Don't confuse your motivations here. Getting-to-know-you conversations should be organic and could just as easily be about your hobbies or where you shop.

'But, as soon as I learn the terminology, the language moves on.' Don't worry. It's the same for everybody. As the authors of this book, we're incredibly aware of our identities but, despite our business involvement in sourcing diverse talent, we all have to keep tuned in to the dynamic nature of changing language, as the world learns how to work effectively with diversity.

MICROAGGRESSION

THE TERM: author of two books on the subject, psychology Professor Derald Wing Sue defines microaggressions as 'the everyday slights, indignities, put-downs and insults that people of color, women, LGBT populations or those who are marginalized experience in their day-to-day interactions with people'.[5]

WHAT IT IS: a term first proposed by psychiatrist Chester M. Pierce in the 1970s,[6] designed to provide a common vocabulary for people to talk about a specific type of daily indignities they face due to implicit biases in society.

CORE IDEA: highlighting the type of actions or comments that are painful to a person because they have to do with that person's membership in a group discriminated against.

AIMS: making it public knowledge that seemingly small and innocent offenses are harmful and can lead to anger and depression and lower work productivity and efficiency.

WHERE IT'S GOING: appearing more and more in the workplace to raise awareness of how such behavior can make the environment more hostile and less validating and inclusive.

FIVE COMMON MICROAGGRESSIONS

- 'So, tell me, where are you actually from?'

- 'When I look at you, I don't see color.'

- 'You are so articulate.'

- 'As a woman, I know what you go through as a racial minority.'

- 'Everyone can succeed in this society, if they work hard enough.'

While there's some language around race to learn and appreciate, there's no need to get bogged down in notions of political correctness. Bear in mind that it's difficult to have conversations with people without all trying to speak the same language and respecting some boundaries.

When it comes to race in the workplace and in society, silence and avoidance are not the answers for any of us. There's a learning curve here for everybody. Put in the effort and you'll get over it.

Let's imagine a Q&A session between us and a white manager who wants to learn . . .

Can I say 'Black'?

Yes, as long as you're aware that it can mean different things in different places. Sometimes 'Black' is used as an umbrella term for a range of non-white ethnic-minority populations. More commonly, though, it describes people of African and Caribbean descent, who may also identify as 'West-Indian American', 'Afro-Caribbean', 'African American' or (outside of the US) 'Black British', 'Afro-German' etc. There is important context and experience that aligns with each of these backgrounds.

Then I can use 'Black, Asian and Minority Ethnic' – BAME?

Yes, you can, as long as you're aware that this is one of those terms that's becoming increasingly seen as a detrimental part of the problem by Black people. This term is common in the UK where, in recent times, BAME has been used to refer to people who are not white. But not everyone belonging to this group wants to be included in one homogenous mass. They may be of mixed race or come from a number of different ethnicities. It gives permission to glaze over the variety of specific issues different ethnic groups might face in the workplace and beyond – crudely lumping solutions and approaches together under a single 'non-white' grouping, as though all ethnic minorities have identical experiences and therefore one size fits all.

So should I use 'colored' instead?

No. This is definitely an old-fashioned and offensive term that can sound naive or patronizing in a multi-ethnic environment, suggesting that color is an attribute possessed by all skin types except white. The same applies to 'half-caste' – a better term to use is 'mixed race' or 'people of color' (POC).

But haven't I heard the term 'people of color' in use?

Yes, 'people of color' has been the preferred collective term for referring to people of non-white racial groups in the US. Like BAME, the phrase is slipping into the past. For the time being, you may find better reception for it when you use it alongside the name that identifies a specific racial group. For example, African American, American Indian, Hispanic or Latinx.

What does BIPOC mean?

The acronym BIPOC refers to 'Black, Indigenous and other People Of Color' and aims to emphasize the historic oppression of Black and indigenous people.[7] Umbrella labels can be detrimental to specific communities, especially the Black community. More on this later.

Wouldn't it be better not to see color at all?

No. This is often the mistake that well-meaning white liberals make when they want to address ethnic diversity. Race and color are part of everyone's identity. It's important to acknowledge and embrace identity, rather than diminish its importance for fear of saying the wrong thing. If in doubt, just ask the question.

I'm confused. Surely identity is about being different, not inclusive?

Again, this is one of the dilemmas that trouble us when we think about diversity of any kind. Not all people over fifty struggle with technology, not all Millennials are lazy and complacent and not all women choose to have a family. We're so used to binary choices – either/or. What about both/and? The point here is that we show we're inclusive by recognizing and embracing difference. The easier it is to spot ethnic identity different to our own, the sooner we can acknowledge it.

Why shouldn't we use umbrella labels for race?

Labels can be damaging and, while useful in some cases, it's important to consider the potential harm they can have on ethnic minorities in the workplace. Race and ethnicity are topics that a lot of (white) people just aren't comfortable talking about. Using a term like BAME or POC allows the topic to be brought up, while perhaps not acknowledging the level of nuance necessary to have meaningful conversations.

Surely umbrella terms can be useful in some ways?
Grouping ethnicities can ignore the intricacies and nuances of multiple cultures. People of different ethnicity have vastly different experiences that cannot be encompassed in such restrictive terms. BAME, POC or BIPOC are quick-fix labels that group huge numbers of people together under one umbrella, allowing businesses to view 'diversity' as a box-ticking exercise, when they've hired 'a person of color'. Hiring one Indian man to the board doesn't mean there might not be barriers for Black women in your business. The terms have their place, but we must be cautious about when to speak about a specific person and when to speak about a group.

When We Talk About Representation . . .

We have to make sure we're taking in the full demography of the workforce. The US census offers eight categories to identify for Race and Hispanic Origin.[8] In the UK, the ONS uses eighteen official ethnic classifications for the UK census – there is no one 'BAME box' to tick.[9]

Having true diversity is important and yields better results – inclusive teams make better business decisions 87% of the time.[10]

So how come not enough is being done internally to support different cultures or backgrounds?

When designing diversity policies and interventions, companies need to make sure the needs and desires of specific groups are being listened to. Having employee networks to support different groups can help shape company culture and put pressure on leadership to create more inclusive policies and environments. It's crucial to ensure that these networks take into account numerous cultures and backgrounds, and don't just focus on one ethnic group, thereby excluding others.

In summary, it's mostly about context:

- Umbrella terms like BAME, POC or BIPOC are useful when speaking about ethnically diverse talent in areas such as the ethnicity pay gap – or to refer to a broader inclusion strategy

- Such terms can be divisive, however, as they force all ethnically diverse people into a single grouping and 'presume' they have the same experience

- Whenever you can, be specific: for instance, when speaking about BLM, and its impact on your workforce, always say 'Black inclusion' or 'Black talent'

- When you need to speak about various groups, 'ethnically diverse' can be a better term to use, as it avoids making any group or ethnicity the 'other'.

WANT TO KNOW MORE?

To get a sense of the different cultural histories and their importance today, it's worth checking out both American and British sources listed in our Further Resources section.

Given that systemic racism has been taking place in our societies for centuries, there are regular new developments, changes, turnarounds and lots of nuances to come to terms with.

For this and contemporary book titles on subjects like 'cancel culture', head to page 241.

POSITIVE ACTION

OPENING UP DIFFICULT CONVERSATIONS AT PWC

If it's so difficult to talk about race in the workplace that it never happens, how can we even think about solutions? In 2017, members of PwC's Multicultural Business Network (MBN) in London asked themselves many such questions. Determined to break this, MBN launched the #ColourBrave Campaign – a multi-channel initiative to increase visibility of ethnic minorities at PwC and encourage conversations addressing challenges faced by these communities.[11] Including a portrait exhibition, the training of champions and ambassadors, as well as a guide to stimulate dialogue about race, ColourBrave led to PwC developing a more open culture through greater engagement and the publishing of the company's ethnicity pay-gap data.

NASDAQ ASKS COMPANIES TO DIVERSIFY OR DELIST

After finding that more than 75% of its listed companies did not meet its proposed diversity requirements, Nasdaq adopted a new requirement for the 3,249 companies listed on its main US stock exchange: have at least one woman and one 'diverse' director and report data on board diversity – or face consequences. This means Nasdaq now requires boards to have at least one woman and one director who self-identifies as an under-represented minority or LGBT+. Companies that don't disclose diversity information face potential delisting, while those that report their data but don't meet the standards will have to publicly explain why. Nasdaq cites research showing the benefits of board diversity, from higher-quality financial disclosures to the lower likelihood of audit problems.[12]

GRAPPLING WITH 'WOKE'
AND 'CANCEL' CULTURE

There's an elephant in the room here. We don't want to have to call people out on their biases. Yet, as leaders in the workplace, we are responsible for managing and encouraging respectful relationships around us. How can we possibly do that without blaming, shaming and, yes, 'canceling' people? Who wouldn't be anxious about this?

The Culture of 'Woke' and 'Canceling'

Like 'political correctness', the term 'woke' originated for good reasons – to support a more aware and non-judgemental view of others. Yet, in a very short time, 'woke' has come to mean the opposite, often used by people to accuse someone of calling out others with the wrong intentions and 'canceling' them. So much so that 'woke' itself is even being weaponized as a pejorative term. One person's social justice is another's social pain.

We've all heard of 'cancel culture', the social-media-fueled public shaming of individuals for perceived transgressions current and historical. Once you've been named and shamed in this way, everything you say and do is scrutinized for you to fail over and over again. As Kendall Jenner discovered when she breezily attempted to bridge the gap between protestors and police by offering up a soda and inadvertently trivialized the entire BLM movement.[13]

On either side of any debate, nobody likes 'cancel culture' and everybody fears being 'canceled'. Like 'woke', according to the *New York Times*, 'canceling' is a term that originated in Black culture and has been misappropriated and weaponized to demonize anyone whose opinion we don't like. Around the time of the 2020 US presidential election, books on 'cancel culture' were jumping off the presses. There are even media charts of the greatest 'woke' victims of 2020.

Barack Obama: *'I do get a sense sometimes now, among certain young people . . . of: "The way of me making change is to be as judgemental as possible about other people." "I can sit back and feel pretty good about myself, because man, you see how woke I was? I called you out." This idea of purity, and you're never compromised, and you're always politically woke and all that stuff, you should get over that quickly. The world is messy.'*[14]

We get it. It's why we wrote this book.

#BLACKLIVESMATTER MATTERS

We cannot have a discussion about race without talking about Black Lives Matter, the movement started in 2013 in response to the acquittal of Trayvon Martin's murderer.

George Zimmerman decided, against the instructions of police, to pursue an unarmed Black teenager through a Florida gated community because of his supposed resemblance to African American burglars in the area. Police failed to arrest Zimmerman for shooting Martin dead, accepting his claim that he acted in self-defense.

The color-blind narrative dominated the trial and the judge forbade any mention of 'racial profiling'. Zimmerman's lawyers argued that race played no role in Zimmerman's actions because he had not expressed racial animus towards Martin in police interviews, assuming that 'racism' can only refer to meetings of the Ku Klux Klan or New Black Panther Party.

GERRYMANDER

/ˈdʒɛrɪˌmandə/

gerund or present participle: gerrymandering

manipulate the boundaries of (an electoral constituency) so as to favor one party or class.

achieve (a result) by gerrymandering.

'an attempt to gerrymander the election result'[16]

Founded by activist Alicia Garza,[15] BLM has generated an extraordinary amount of energy. Whether you believe this to be shining a much-needed light on 400 years of oppression, or you fear the social unrest that has emerged as a result of the movement, the systemic racism we still witness is indisputable.

The so-called Jim Crow laws – redlining and gerrymandering that enforced racial segregation or suppression in the United States – still have a huge impact on those communities today. These were any of the laws that sanctioned racial segregation in the American South between the end of Reconstruction in 1877 and the beginning of the civil rights movement in the 1950s.

In its Plessy v. Ferguson decision (1896), the US Supreme Court ruled that 'separate but equal' facilities for African Americans did not violate the Fourteenth Amendment, ignoring evidence that the facilities for Black people were inferior to those intended for whites.[17] This created a racial wealth gap and disparities in investment into critical services like education and lack of access to financial and other services. Gerrymandering restricted the voice of these communities to impact positive change.[18] These practices have meant that the Black and minority communities affected have had to play catch-up through multiple generations. If you have not taken the time to read up on this, then we highly recommend it (see Further Resources: Race, page 241).

The BLM protests of summer 2020 were an awakening moment for everyone in the world. The cruel murder of George Floyd at the hands of a police officer was horrific to see. It was a reminder that this was not an isolated occurrence but it exposed us all to the systemic racism faced by the Black community, specifically in America, though the impact was felt across the globe. #BlackLivesMatter leaves many white people feeling uncomfortable and unsettled. It hurts to be told that, as a white person, you are effectively collaborating with a racist society. But it hurts far more to be on the receiving end of that collaboration as a Black person experiencing systemic state violence and marginalization, so think carefully about how you respond to your discomfort.

'White fragility' is a term used to encapsulate the defensiveness, clumsiness and anger that white people often display when confronted with matters of race that make them feel uneasy. Instead of focusing on solving the problem, they focus on their own feelings. We highly recommend reading Robin DiAngelo's *White Fragility: Why It's So Hard for White People to Talk About Racism* to learn more about this topic.

BLM is:

• about equity in systems and institutions

• overhauling corrupt institutions, such as policing

• collaboration and action from white people to review, critique and overhaul the systems they control.

BLM isn't:

• about elevating any one race over another

• wanting white people to feel guilty

• about Black people solving the challenges alone.

As difficult as it may seem, nothing has expedited progress towards recent racial equity more than the Black Lives Matter movement. If this isn't a topic for discussion in your workplace, what is? Ask Marc Benioff.

A LEADER GETS SERIOUS ABOUT WELCOMING RACIAL DIVERSITY IN HIS WORKPLACE

MARC BENIOFF, FOUNDER & CEO, SALESFORCE

In July 2016, Alton Sterling, an unarmed Black man, was fatally shot at close range by two white police officers in Baton Rouge, Louisiana. The following day, another Black man, Philando Castile, was pulled over in Falcon Heights, Minnesota, and shot and killed in front of his girlfriend and four-year-old daughter by a white police officer. Unfortunately, these tragic incidents were part of long-standing systemic racism that more recently echoed throughout the world in mass protests over the murder of George Floyd in May of 2020 by a white police officer.

During the incidents in 2016, I tweeted a photo of Black Lives Matter activist DeRay Mckesson on his knees being arrested during a protest. He wore a T-shirt that said '#staywoke', with a Black version of the Twitter bird logo on the front. I'd always admired Twitter's employee resource group for Black employees, which they call Black Birds (the company's equivalent of our company's BOLDforce). So the next day I tweeted, 'Yes that is a @Twitter @Blackbirds logo. Amazing to see tech as a vehicle for social change. Respect.'

It took me a few seconds to realize that my comment touting tech as a vehicle for social change was completely tone-deaf in that moment.

Replies poured in, slamming me for hypocrisy and worse. The general view was that someone like me, a CEO in an industry plagued by a terrible record of hiring Black employees, had no right to wrap himself around a movement aimed at combating racism. The criticism was absolutely fair. Black employees made up just over 2% of our workforce in the United States, and fewer than 4% were Hispanic or Latinx. That's not nearly representative of the communities where we live and work.

This experience was gutting. I apologized individually to nearly every person who commented on the post, but I was seriously rattled. How could I have thought, even for a second, that this was a reasonable way to show support for racial justice? I'd made the mistake of picking up a megaphone to champion a cause, when I should have been focusing on getting my own house in order.

I reached out to Molly Ford, who worked on our public-relations team, to ask her what her experience has been as a Black woman working at Salesforce. She told me that she didn't believe there was enough effort being made to help others understand the struggles of under-represented communities. Molly quoted an old saying to me: 'Shepherds do not beget sheep. Sheep beget sheep' – meaning if we were serious about becoming a welcoming place, we had to bring more racial *diversity into our ranks, and we needed to give our employees from under-represented groups a better way to broach issues that impacted them. We'd have to start all over by looking in the mirror again.*

I took her advice to heart, and Salesforce committed even more to helping close the opportunity divide and giving young people facing barriers to success a path to meaningful careers by donating funds and employee time to underserved local schools. Since 2013, Salesforce employees have adopted more than a hundred schools globally, and thirty-four schools in San Francisco and Oakland, and our global education investment now totals more than $120 million.

We work with organizations such as PepUp Tech, a non-profit that provides underserved students access, skills and mentorship to begin careers in tech. We also partnered with organizations, such as Year Up, that provide young adults with high-demand vocational job skills, experience and support. Our Futureforce global recruiting program, which we introduced in 2014, is focused on attracting to Salesforce a diverse pool of university graduates and urban youth, as well as veterans and their spouses.

We aspire to have 50% of our US workforce made up of under-represented groups (women, Black, Latinx, indigenous, multiracial, LGBTQ+, people with disabilities, and veterans) by 2023 and to continue building a workplace that reflects society around the globe. And now – in response to the most recent incidents of racial inequality and injustices – we've also announced an additional goal of doubling our US representation of Black employees in leadership roles.

I believe that business is the greatest platform for change, and that we have a responsibility to create a more equal workforce and world. Whether it's advocating for racial equality, gender equality or LGBTQ+ equality, I've learned it starts with listening deeply and asking questions. And then, once we have a deeper understanding, we need to act with compassion, we need to work together with our communities to bring about positive change.

Salesforce is a cloud-based software company listed on the New York Stock Exchange and has over 60,000 employees globally and revenues of over $20 billion.

HOW TO KEEP AWAY FROM NEGATIVE LANGUAGE

Are you clear in yourself about the inclusion of ethnically diverse talents in discussions at work? If you're not, it's important that you work at it. Check in with yourself. Try the following.

Word Association Exercise

Rather than a one-off exercise, consider this an ongoing experiment about recognizing language that *isn't* inclusive of ethnic minorities.

Come up with a simple and memorable word you'll note to yourself when you hear what you believe to be microaggressions or non-inclusive language in a conversation. Subtle examples would include:

- Repeatedly mispronouncing your colleague's name when they have already corrected you

- Overuse of umbrella terms around race for fear of not being able to say the word 'Black'

- Hearing a non-white colleague specifically called out for how 'articulate' they are

- Assuming a co-worker's emotional response based on their gender, sexual orientation, race or ethnicity.

You're not looking for major infractions here, just nuances. Of course, you'll have to deal with anything major through the appropriate channels. Instead, in this exercise, you're listening for little things: microaggressions, non-inclusive language.

When they occur, keep repeating your memorable word to yourself, in your head.

Debrief

After a week or so, stop and reflect on the occasions you had to fire up this memorable word in your mind. How did it make you feel? Were you surprised at how many times it came up?

Did you find this a useful way to bring immediate attention to negative language?

Do you think this is something you could extend to colleagues, to help them notice microaggressions or non-inclusive language and talk about it as it happens?

Encouraging discussions in your own team about race will become a lot easier when you've made it clear about your personal support for the inclusion of ethnic minorities in conversation.

Making it personal will make a difference. Think about what's motivating you here. Are you passionate about human rights? Do you want to see equal opportunities and equity in your team? Is it the performance of the business that drives you?

If you do it in your own style, and can feel good about showing everyone why the inclusion of ethnic minorities matters to you, you'll have more impact with your team. If you want to see real change in your workplace, being a role model is important. Others will be waiting for you to lead by example.

Using inclusive language is something we're all responsible for; however, why not try something counter-intuitive with your team?

NOT RACIST OR ANTI-RACIST?

There's quite a difference between these points of view and you may have heard 'anti-racist' a lot recently. But what does it mean? Ibram X. Kendi wrote a great book about it which we highly recommend you read – *How to Be an Antiracist* (see Further Resources on page 242). He defines it as: 'one who is supporting an antiracist policy through their actions or expressing an antiracist idea'.

Kendi is saying, 'Not racist? Good. But why simply stand by and watch, when you could be taking action to change mindsets and behavior?' You can become actively anti-racist, by learning about the challenges that racially diverse people experience and doing something about it.

You may not believe you have a racist bone in your body, but the system you live in has it down to the marrow. Kendi suggests six steps:[19]

1. Understand the definition of racist

2. Stop saying, 'I'm not racist'

3. Identify racial inequities and disparities

4. Confront the racist ideas you've been holding

5. Understand how anti-racism works with gender, sexuality and ethnicity

6. Be a champion of anti-racist policies.

WORK THROUGH
EDUCATION FOR EMPATHY

We haven't written a book on the importance of talking about race and how people from ethnic minorities have struggled in the workplace. We have merely touched upon the subject in one chapter of a book on diversity and inclusion.

Even so, we have gone strong on empathy. And, in our experience, you only get to empathy through greater self-awareness. And to self-awareness through education.

Educate yourself. Educate others. Be educated by others. Never stop learning about yourself or others.

There's a dynamic, wonderful, ever-changing and often discombobulating language of race to help you have some challenging and brilliant conversations in your workplace.

Watch out for the tripwires. You don't get to be an expert on 400 years of Black history by reading one book on 'white fragility'. Avoid overloading the one or two Black people in your office with the responsibility of representing and answering for their entire race.

Have those conversations about race anyway. It really is up to you.

GET YOUR ACT TOGETHER

Avoiding conversations about race in the workplace is no longer an option and it's important for you to initiate this dialogue.

Develop your empathy by educating yourself on the issues of race. The history of race and racism in your country is a good place to start.

Get to grips with the ever-changing language of race.

Be more aware of microaggressions and how they affect individuals and the team.

Take your courage in your hands and lose your fear of making mistakes.

NEXT>>>>>   LISTEN TO WHAT WOMEN WANT

CHAPTER 4

LISTEN TO WHAT WOMEN WANT

Women enter the world as equals both in numbers and capacity, yet almost immediately the inequity sneaks in. As this has been happening for centuries, it's now time to change it.

As women grow up, they learn about the power of friends, and girls become inseparable. Until they reach the workforce, take a brief look up, see that there is only one seat at the top and sharpen their elbows. Historically, this sent a clear message: you are not competing against the men in the room, you are competing against the other women!

But the stereotype is becoming obsolete as women come together to dispel this myth and commit to collaboration to drive change. If women support each other and men also serve as effective Allies and sponsors, then gender equity is the inevitable conclusion.

Look around you. If the population has a roughly 50:50 gender split, then why is that not represented in your business as you look up the career ladder? Because your business is not meritocratic.

Years before you joined the workforce, decades even, the

struggle for gender equity was taking place and going through its cycles of awareness and action. And here it is again, before you now. Your thoughts and questions?

> *Didn't we sort out gender equity long before I joined the*
> *company?*
> *Am I being asked to deal with this now because of the*
> *#MeToo movement?*
> *If gender equity is about pay, this is surely one for HR.*
> *We don't still discriminate that way in our organization, do we?*
> *I'm sure I don't hold back opportunities from women in my*
> *team.*

One of the most common quotes we hear from clients is that they no longer need to focus on gender equity because they 'have that covered'.

Hmm . . . tell that to the authors of the 2020 Women CEOs in America report,[1] produced by Women Business Collaborative, C200 and Catalyst. Their research told them that there's only gender pay parity between women and men in 20% of companies. Not surprisingly, their campaigning aim is 100% by 2030.

According to the World Economic Forum[2] and a plethora of recent studies (see Further Resources: Women, page 245), our businesses and organizations will neither reach gender equity in our lifetime nor, in all likelihood, our children's.

Shocked? If you're like Unilever CEO Alan Jope, who gives us his experience later in the chapter, you will be. But then, we all should be. More to the point, what can you do about this?

Start by familiarizing yourself with the latest research on gender equity, certainly. But by far the best thing you can do is to listen to what women say about what they experience in terms of gender inequity and what they want to change.

Your learning curve may be steep, but it's one that will alter the way you think and act forever.

THE NUMBERS ARE ILLUMINATING

- An alarming 42% of women in the US experience gender discrimination at work.[3]

- Comparative stats from the Human Capital Hub[4] show that, in 2018, victims of sex-based discrimination received more than $148 million in payouts from the complaints.

- Both men and women are twice as likely to hire a male candidate.

- Women are seventy-nine times[5] more likely to be hired when there are at least two female candidates in the finalist pool.

- Half of men believe women are well represented at their company, when 90% of senior leaders are men.

- Significantly, 40% of men and women now notice a double standard against female candidates.

- Men view unconscious bias as the number-one barrier women face in their careers.

- Men are 30% more likely to obtain managerial roles.

- Women and men ask for pay raises at the same rate. Women receive pay raises 5% less often.

- Some 4% of C-suite roles are held by women of color.

DISCOVER WHAT WOMEN EXPERIENCE

The Fortune 500 shows that women hold only thirty-eight CEO positions (7.6%) and women of color hold less than a single percent (August 2020).[6]

Only 5% of the FTSE 100 CEOs are women and there are no women of color CEOs (March 2020).[7]

With women accounting for 50% of the world population, there's no excuse for still not having an equal share of the opportunities available in the business world. Yet progress in this space has been glacial and some of the questions and statements ambitious women face are anything but equitable:

How do you balance work and family?
This role will force you to make tough decisions – can you handle that?
You come across as a little too aggressive.
What does your husband think about you taking this role?

GENDER EQUITY IS EVERYONE'S BUSINESS

It doesn't take a genius to spot the theme that a focus on family seems to denote lack of commitment or split loyalty. Far more preferable would be a theme of equal partnership in parenting, or the ability to make your own choices on prioritizing personal and professional commitments. Aren't these matters everyone's business?

You're probably wondering how to operate when #MeToo is fresh in everyone's minds. Every frontline campaign brings a backlash reaction. Is it best now for men to keep their heads down and not expose themselves to any risk? Have we now come full circle from eighteenth-century protocols, where single women needed a chaperone when meeting a man?

The #MeToo movement was simply asking for men to behave as decent human beings in the workplace and society, so what is your role in seeing that this happens? While calling out bad behavior when you see it is a clear duty for you, how do you even know that you're seeing it? If he missed the cues, then you might have missed them too . . .

Then, what happens when you, a man, call out another man? Does this sound disingenuous? Are you speaking out where women should speak out? Is that 'canceling'?

Ever spotted that little microaggression all too familiar to many women in the workplace – that it's important for a female leader to be likable, but it doesn't really matter for men? And, admit it, how many times have you been relieved when a woman in your team offers to take the notes in a meeting?

What about the other historical ways you yourself have behaved around women? Have you used the word 'mankind' as a general term that assumes men are the most important of the human race? Have you talked about being castrated or having 'no balls', as a sign of losing power, because being more feminine would make you weak?

Just because there are more questions than answers does not mean that you must avoid the issue of gender equity through fear of failure. Or, worse, being called out for misbehavior yourself. We come back to the topic of education. Start with learning about some of the inequity that we know is prevalent, like the gender pay gap for instance.

GENDER PAY GAP

THE TERM: The gender pay gap can be defined as the difference between the median hourly earnings of men and of women. This is distinct from equal pay, which refers to men and women in the same job earning an equal wage.[8]

WHAT IT IS: In 2019 the gender pay gap was 17.3% in the UK, which means that, on average, women were paid approximately 83p for every £1 men were paid. In the US in 2020, women made only $0.81 for every dollar a man made.

CORE IDEA: By calculating presumptive raises given over a forty-year career, we find that women stand to lose $900,000 on average over a lifetime.

AIMS: By calculating your gender pay gap, you're learning the level of female representation at the top needs to improve to close the gap. The gender pay gap now extends beyond the notion of 'equal pay for equal work', largely because it reduces economic output and means that women are more likely to be dependent upon welfare payments.

WHERE IT'S GOING: Awareness of the gender pay gap increases women's access to higher-paying jobs by promoting an inclusive recruiting process that doesn't discriminate on the basis of gender. The pay gap is beginning to expand to ethnicity too so that ethnically diverse talent can have access to high-paying jobs in business.

FACILITATE AND LEARN

Your task from now on is to listen to what women want. Do this by being an Ally to them and enabling discussions that draw in all employees. The first step is to see women as individuals who all have different aspirations and goals. For instance, assuming that all women want a family is the same as assuming all men are misogynists.

Draw attention to the work of groups like Catalyst, with their phenomenal #BiasCorrect campaign[9] that highlighted some of the labels women are given, showing how these can be such an invisible yet powerful barrier for women in the workplace.

For example, if a man is not afraid to display strong feelings or beliefs, people say he is 'passionate'. Yet, when a woman does the same, people say she is 'emotional'.

The content is the same. The label is different. It is gender bias and it's ingrained in the workplace and in society. If we all do it, we can all learn not to do it. If, that is, we want to achieve gender equity.

WANT TO KNOW MORE?

For links to organizations like Catalyst, the 30% Club and Women Business Collaborative, as well as pointers to the latest research and stats on gender issues, like Women CEOs of America, please **go to Further Resources, page 245.**

HUBSPOT SHOWS INBOUND MARKETING IS FEMALE-FRIENDLY TOO

Recognized for the way it championed inbound marketing that doesn't interrupt customers, HubSpot is also now known for being a frequent winner of best-place-to-work awards, often due to its female-friendly benefit packages.[10] The company states in its mission that business can grow with a conscience and succeed with a soul. With three female board members, HubSpot includes sixteen weeks of paid parental leave and family planning benefits, flexible and remote work arrangements and unlimited time off.

THE 30% CLUB DRIVES BOARD DIVERSITY IN THE UK AND BEYOND

The 30% Club is a global campaign led by chairs and CEOs taking action to increase gender diversity at board and senior management levels. It was originally founded by a good friend of ours, Dame Helena Morrissey, back in 2010, when board diversity for women sat at 12% in the FTSE 100. Due to the campaign's interventions, it now sits at over 35% across the FTSE 350. By focusing on the largely straight white men at the top and using data to drive change, the 30% Club achieved an incredible result. There are now chapters across the world driving this much-needed change at board level for women.

START TAKING ACTION

- Make a topic of conversation the double standard that says whatever a man does a woman has to do better.

- Set up a debate to debunk the philosophy that women compete more with each other than their male counterparts.

- Make a point of asking men about their children, encouraging colleagues to take their paternity leave and maintain balance.

- Introduce the ideas of influential organizations like Women Business Collaborative or the 30% Club, which have emerged to use their collective influence to drive towards equal position, pay and power for all businesswomen.

A BUSINESS LEADER COMES TO UNDERSTAND GENDER EQUITY

ALAN JOPE, CEO, UNILEVER

Growing up in 1960s and 1970s Glasgow, sectarianism was more present than any form of inclusion. We had, and continue to have, a shocking fracture along religious grounds. I had been out of Glasgow for nine years, including five years living in the melting pot of 1980s London, when my wife and I moved with Unilever to the Eastern United States, just outside New York. By then I felt that I had progressed to carrying an open mindset on matters of gender, race, sexual orientation and so on. However, moving to the US was a real wake-up call that my attitudes and skills were still in the Dark Ages. Over time I learned – sometimes the hard way.

Back in the UK, I got into argument after argument with friends who tried to run down what they labeled as 'American political correctness'. This contrast between the two sides of the Atlantic was an eye-opener. What I once had found funny, I now found inappropriate, chauvinist and wrong.

Moving to China in 2009 was a new learning curve. Chairman Mao – founder of the People's Republic of China and leader of its Communist Party – had declared that 'women hold up half the sky' and, indeed, our company was really run by a cohort of amazing women middle managers. That cohort now makes up the leadership team of Unilever's business in China – and it is a source of real pride for me that we have held the door open for Jennice, Wai-Fung, Daphne, Ying, Jennifer, Joy and many others to reach top leadership positions.

The privilege of being white, male, European and a CEO is enormous. We are the elephant in the room . . . and must never forget that.

Unilever is a multinational consumer goods company listed on the London Stock Exchange, with 150,000 employees globally and turnover of €51 billion.

IT'S BEEN STARING US ALL IN THE FACE

Giving women the support they need to take advantage of opportunities does not mean overlooking others. Equity is everyone's business. We must view this process as the rising tide that lifts ALL ships.

Any cursory observation reveals that everybody balances family loyalties and workplace commitment, not just women. Are we going to continue to make assumptions about a woman's request for flexibility vs a man's request?

A small shift to volunteering our views on flexibility/parental policies for both men and women alike will quickly break down dated stereotypes. With men as genuine Allies for gender equity at work, we benefit from the unique viewpoint presented by 50% of the population, i.e. women, that control over $20 trillion in worldwide spending.[11]

THERE IS A WAY FORWARD

If your company, alongside other organizations, can see the problems facing gender equity in a time of great economic pressure, it can help female employees overcome barriers and encourage the whole workforce to be more flexible.

1. **Keep it real.** The company needs to consider revising the productivity and performance expectations, goals

and deadlines set before pandemic and economic downturns. For working mothers, senior-level women and many employees, burnout is a serious problem, requiring creative solutions.

2. **Be even more flexible.** With more remote working and the boundaries between home and work blurring, this is an opportunity to think about establishing new and different boundaries, particularly around flexible work options, and adjusting policies and programs to recognize the need to better support employees.

3. **Look at gender bias again.** All these dramatic changes faced by workplaces mean that women may be experiencing gender bias more now than they have in recent times. For example, four times as many women as men dropped out of the labor force in September 2020,[12] validating predictions that the COVID-19 pandemic had a more negative impact on professional women with its accompanying childcare and school crises. Companies need to help people be more aware than ever about taking steps to minimize gender bias.

4. **Communicate openly and often.** It would be easy during economic crises for any company to forget to keep its employees informed of what is happening, when every decision has an impact on people's jobs. Difficult news needs communicating with careful planning.

This is the bigger picture. Now, what comes next is down to you.

HOW YOU CAN PERSONALLY MAKE PROGRESS ON GENDER EQUITY

If you're now open to seeing that a subject you might have considered 'covered' is far away from where it needs to be, you're thinking along very positive lines.

In place of a practical exercise, here are some useful questions you can ask yourself and steps you can take from this point on to show that you are an Ally for gender equity in your workplace.

- **Gender pay-gap reporting** – are you aware what your organization is doing about this?

- **#MeToo backlash** – who can help you take practical steps that support and educate men?

- **Celebrating women's achievements** – are you talking about these?

- **Parental leave** – are you making sure that men, women and all parents in your team are taking it?

- **Intersectional women** – how are you including all women? Women of color? Gay women?

GET YOUR ACT TOGETHER

Women want what they're due in the workplace – equal consideration for work opportunities, promotions, leadership and travel.

Like men, women are individuals who all have different aspirations and goals, so avoid assumptions based on gender stereotypes and ask everyone what their goals are.

Everybody has a life outside of work, not just women, so remove the stigma that only women need flexibility by giving permission to all your employees to have flexibility without being penalized – they will be more productive for you when they have balance.

Avoid the #MeToo backlash – Allies and advocates are as important now as they have ever been, so work on the assumption that most women are not waiting to spring you with a lawsuit.

Support gender equity by celebrating women's achievements.

NEXT>>>>>   GET TO KNOW YOUR LGBT+
COLLEAGUES

CHAPTER 5

GET TO KNOW YOUR LGBT+ COLLEAGUES

When did you know you were straight? Yes, you've probably always known. So why would it be any different for someone who is gay? Being LGBT+ is not a choice.

Can you imagine a workplace in which you have to give a false pronoun for your partner, through fear of people knowing you are straight (see page 108)? Then having to remember to keep doing that, time and time again, to avoid conflict?

Reminding themselves to change the pronoun of their partner and constantly having to say it incorrectly are unfortunately the everyday practices of closeted LGBT+ people at work. You may recall that more than half of LGBT+ workers hide their sexual orientation in the workplace.

If you've spent your working life to date calling people either 'he' or 'she' with no exceptions, you've only been doing what the vast majority of your colleagues have done.

We use the term LGBT+ rather than LGBT or LGBTQ or LGBTQIA. We believe that LGBT+ is a more inclusive term to use as there are so many letters after the T representing different communities and identities that it can get confusing and very long to list them all. We may deviate from this at some point if the research we're referencing uses a different term. More on the different letters later in this chapter.

Now, to include everyone in your team and organization, you're becoming aware that you have to find and use a whole new, non-binary vocabulary.

Whether you currently lead a team or are an individual contributor, people are looking to you to say and do the right thing.

Reading these words may be causing you some concern right now. If you're having a conversation with yourself like this one below, it's perfectly reasonable . . .

I'm very uncomfortable about doing this.
Everybody around me is uncomfortable about it.
They're all waiting to follow my lead.
It's far easier to get this wrong than right.
I'm tempted to say and do nothing.
How do I even begin to ask the question?
What if I misgender someone or use the wrong words?

Well, the honest truth is that you will take one giant step in the right direction by getting to know your LGBT+ colleagues better. Simple changes to everyday language can make a huge difference to those around you.

Working with all kinds of organizations on diversity, we know it's challenging to change the way you speak and the words you use, but getting it right pays dividends. Later in the chapter, Virgin Group founder Richard Branson explains how years of

dedication to continual improvement enabled his LGBT+ colleagues to see his company as their family and support system.

WHY SHOULD THIS MATTER TO ME?

Did you know it's illegal to be LGBT+ in seventy countries around
the world?[1] Worse than that, twelve of these countries have the
death penalty for it. Can you imagine fearing for your life for simply being who you are?

The ILGA State-Sponsored Homophobia report, released in
December 2019, also finds that within UN states:

- 1 in 5 (34, 18%) have legal provisions that restrict the right to
  freedom of expression on LGBT+ issues

- 1 in 5 (41, 22%) have legal provisions that prohibit the
  registration or operation of organizations that work on sexual
  orientation issues

- Only 3 in 10 (57, 30%) have laws offering broad protection from
  discrimination based on sexual orientation (in goods and
  services, education, health, employment)

- Only 2 in 5 (77, 40%) have laws protecting from workplace
  discrimination based on sexual orientation

- Only 1 in 4 (46, 24%) impose enhanced criminal penalties for
  offenses motivated by hate – known to many as 'hate crimes' –
  towards the victim's sexual orientation.

This does not paint a pretty picture of the state of affairs for LGBT+ globally.

Did you also know that you could be fired for being LGBT+ in twenty-seven states in the USA?[2] Yes, you read that right – TWENTY-SEVEN STATES! This was before the Supreme Court ruled in June 2020 that it would be illegal for businesses across the nation to fire employees based on their sexual orientation or gender identity. While one of President Biden's first actions in 2021 was to make it possible once again for the transgender community to serve in the military,[3] we find it shocking that it took so long to afford LGBT+ people the same rights and protections as their heterosexual counterparts in a country with a long-established democracy.

All this oppression, domestically and internationally, makes it more challenging for the community to come out and be themselves. This is where role modeling can help significantly. Remember that being LGBT+ is invisible. You can't see it. You have to choose to declare it and let people know. At INvolve, we publish global role-model lists called OUTstanding, EMpower and HEROes that celebrate the different communities of LGBT+, ethnically diverse and women executives and future leaders, as well as the Allies for each community.[4] These help to challenge stereotypes around where these diverse professionals sit, all while inspiring the next generation. More importantly, and especially for LGBT+, it shows that they are not alone. There are other LGBT+ leaders who are super-successful and driving inclusion in their businesses and beyond regardless of their sexuality or gender identity.

What Can We Do About International LGBT+ Inclusion?

With knowing some of the facts about the danger LGBT+ communities face in some countries, companies have to take extra steps to support them safely. Here is how global organizations are moving between different models, as they engage on LGBT+ issues:[5]

MODEL	PROS	CONS
When in Rome Companies adhere to local norms by creating exceptions to their pro-LGBT policies.	A practical approach in locations where LGBT people face significant legal or safety risks. Allows companies to avoid potential backlash from local governments or entities.	While better than nothing in an anti-LGBT climate, the approach does nothing to foster a sense of inclusion for LGBT employees.
Embassy Companies create an inclusive workplace internally for their LGBT employees without	A possible approach in more moderate locations where the legal or cultural climate is unwelcoming to	While the model enables companies to support LGBT talent, it doesn't address the conditions that

seeking to change laws or social attitudes.

LGBT people, but not overtly hostile.

Enables the adoption of a non-discrimination policy, training on LGBT topics and sponsoring of social activities for LGBT employees.

lead to LGBT exclusion in the first place, meaning employees continue to face discrimination outside the walls of the embassy.

Advocate

Businesses go beyond internal LGBT inclusion and strive to influence the local climate.

A common approach in moderate-to-friendly places, e.g. hundreds of companies lobbied for marriage equality in the United States.

Also possible in more challenging locations, e.g. when businesses successfully lobbied for marriage equality in Taiwan, or when Deutsche Bank boycotted

If a company wants to be a market leader on LGBT inclusion – to recruit and retain LGBT talent, to appeal to LGBT consumers and Allies, and to help create vibrant inclusive economies – it should strive to become an advocate globally.

However, the model is not without risk: it can provoke

Brunei-owned hotels after the country introduced anti-gay laws. In practice, means engaging in activities such as lobbying the government, participating in Pride events and supporting activists.	governments and communities and upset current or potential customers.

While the differences in approach are clear, how can organizations move along towards advocacy?

From When in Rome to Embassy	Focus on the concept of Allyship: in the first month that the EY Global Delivery Services business launched its LGBT Ally network in India, it saw 4,000 of its 21,000 people sign up as Allies. Raise awareness: Dow Brazil offered 'Diversity 101' education to introduce employees to foundational LGBT concepts and, in China, the company gave explanations of every word, such as 'How do you define bisexual? How do you define queer?' Use technology: at Microsoft in India, employees attended an initial LGBT inclusion

event primarily via an anonymous Skype call. Soon after, the company held another fireside chat, which had 'more people in person in the room than on Skype, willing to ask questions fearlessly'.

From Embassy to Advocate	Strengthen the Employee Resource Group: while, in most large organizations, the ERG is the primary vehicle for internal champions to advocate for LGBT inclusion, a Microsoft manager in the UK observed that one of his biggest challenges was finding people to maintain the ERG, which makes leadership succession planning critical.
	Forge external coalitions: Dow, EY and Microsoft recently joined more than 200 businesses by signing onto a US Supreme Court amicus brief to show support for protecting LGBT people from discrimination under existing federal civil rights law.
	Engage in Embassy–Advocacy: identifying internal actions that drive towards the advocate model without fully embracing it can be important, e.g. after Singapore prohibited foreign companies from funding the local LGBT 'Pink Dot' festival, Dow hosted its own internal 'Pink Dot Day'.

What Does Discrimination or Harassment for the LGBT+ Community Look Like in the Workplace?

It might be . . .

- Promoting people of one sexual orientation over those from another

- Giving preferential treatment, such as more desirable positions, roles or tasks to those of a specific orientation

- Reviewing or assessing those of a certain sexual orientation more harshly than other workers, for no reason other than their orientation

- Bullying, threatening, disparaging, insulting people based on orientation

- Discriminating in any way you can think of, based on an assumed orientation.[6]

STILL BELIEVE THAT LGBT+ EMPLOYEES FACE LITTLE OR NO HOSTILITY IN THE WORKPLACE?

Catalyst offers us some mind-boggling statistics:[7]

- In China, 21% of transgender employees reported that they were harassed, bullied or experienced discrimination at work.

- Think it's any different in the US? One-fifth (20%) of LGBT+ Americans have experienced discrimination based on sexual orientation or gender identity when applying for jobs.

- LGBT+ people of color (32%) are more likely to experience this type of discrimination than white LGBT+ people (13%).

- Hard to believe, but 22% of LGBT+ Americans have not been paid equally or promoted at the same rate as their peers.

- Catalyst reminds us that offensive jokes based on sexual orientation or gender identity are a form of harassment. Over half (53%) of LGBT+ employees heard lesbian and gay jokes at work, while 37% heard bisexual jokes and 41% heard transgender jokes in 2018.

Furthermore, transgender workers are subject to different types of harassment than LGB workers. This includes bathroom accessibility, being deliberately referred to by incorrect pronouns, and having to tolerate inappropriate questions, which can lead to employee disengagement and avoidance.

Q&A

Q: What prevents LGBT+ employees from bringing their full selves to work?

A: Fear.

Facts and stats collide. Catalyst tells us that almost half (46%) of LGBTQ workers in the United States are closeted in the workplace. On the other hand, nearly two-thirds (59%) of non-LGBT+ employees believe it is unprofessional to discuss sexual orientation or gender identity at work.

Are we surprised that LGBT+ people often cover or downplay aspects of their authentic selves, such as hiding personal relationships or changing the way they dress or speak? More than a third (35%) of LGBT+ and slightly more than half (51%) of transgender employees in the UK disguised their identity at work for fear of discrimination.[8]

We're asking you to recognize that employees who spend unnecessary time and energy concealing their sexual orientation and gender identity report feeling exhausted. Not even considering that concealment is not an option for transgender employees who wish to begin transitioning, unless they leave their current employers.

LET'S TALK ABOUT PRONOUNS

Just hearing the right pronouns from you can make all the difference. If you know that someone identifies as he or she, then of course you are free to address them with their preferred pronouns. But here are some good tips for those you don't know of when addressing a broader audience:

INSTEAD OF	TRY
his or hers	theirs
ladies and gentlemen	everyone
lady or man	person
men or women	people
guys	folks

Why Are Pronouns Important?

Before we even learn to speak, we are taught words as pairs and opposites. At school, we are split into boys and girls. As adults, we are greeted as ladies and gentlemen.

For many people, a term like 'ladies and gentlemen' may seem perfectly innocuous, but for those who are trans, gender non-binary, genderfluid or genderqueer, these words can be isolating.

So, many non-binary individuals choose to use 'they', a pronoun that comfortably aligns with their identities. In 2019, 'they' was added to the Merriam-Webster dictionary as a singular, non-binary pronoun. It makes sense and is part of our world.

Team members who have never before heard themselves addressed in the right way in the workplace may now feel included for the first time. Outside of the inevitable mental health benefits of being able to be comfortable in your own skin, this also has an incredibly positive impact on productivity. These changes in language do not make any negative impact at all on other employees, but can be so important for some, so why wouldn't you make the effort?

How about encouraging curiosity by appending your own pronouns as part of your email signature? This is how we use them in our own email signatures:

Suki Sandhu [he, him, his]

Felicity Hassan [she, her, hers].

Easy, right? So this is something you can do after reading this chapter. It might not mean much to you, but it will to your LGBT+ colleagues. Why not also put it after your name on Zoom or Microsoft Teams or on your LinkedIn profile, too?

LISTEN FOR THE DIFFERENCES

Employees are 32% more productive when they're comfortable being 'out' at work.[9]

OK, we all tend to cover up differences of some sort. We might not want our colleagues to know we're single, color-blind, on medication for depression, getting divorced. But who we love, where we come from and who we really are – all are fundamental to our wellbeing. The term 'covering', which we touched on in Chapter 1, is particularly prominent in the LGBT+ community and is something you can help reduce in the workplace.

COVERING

THE TERM: downplaying or hiding certain aspects of yourself, from gender to sexuality, race, mental health or any part of your identity that might be judged as out of favor.

WHAT IT IS: in 2006, Kenji Yoshino, a NY law professor, published *Covering: The Hidden Assault on our Civil Rights,* about the damaging effect covering can have on an individual both personally and professionally.[10]

CORE IDEA: masking who you really are as a person, in order to fit into an environment or group.

AIMS: use of the term recognizes that people do try to avoid being seen as different and attracting negative discrimination.

WHERE IT'S GOING: the term is increasingly used to highlight that, in our diverse society, we are all outside the mainstream in some way and we all 'cover'.

As a leader in your workplace, you are in a position to understand just how different everyone around you actually is.

All anybody is asking is that you become familiar with how different people express their gender and identity, so you can help them be more themselves at work.

Start by understanding the concepts, terms and language in use around gender and identity. While you'll probably have heard some before, note the nuances of meaning now associated with these terms.

Lesbian/gay woman refers to a woman with romantic and/or sexual orientation towards women.

Gay/gay man is a man with romantic and/or sexual orientation towards men.

Bisexual means a romantic and/or sexual orientation towards both men and women; some also consider bisexual to mean a romantic or sexual attraction to one's own gender as well as others – similar to 'pansexual'.

Asexual can mean someone attracted to neither men nor women, or denote someone who is romantically attracted but not sexually.

Other terms will probably be new to you and, while many may sound academic, it's useful to appreciate their meanings.

Cisgender identifies a person whose gender identity aligns with the sex they were assigned at birth.

Gender identity means how you think about yourself, the gender you feel you are.

Gender dysphoria describes a condition in which a person feels distress due to a mismatch between their gender identity and the sex they were assigned at birth.

Gender expression concerns how you demonstrate your gender – through dress, mannerisms, speech and demeanor.

Genderfluid people can experience different gender identities at different times.

Sexual orientation and gender identity

This image is a simplification of the idea of different elements of one's sexual and gender identities as existing on a continuum rather than being binary or fixed.

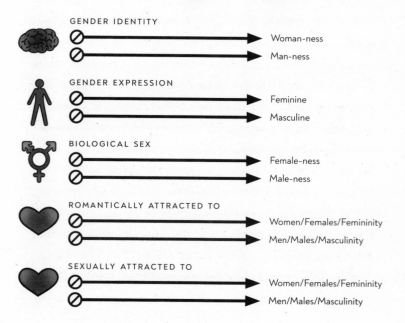

GENDER IDENTITY

Woman-ness

Man-ness

GENDER EXPRESSION

Feminine

Masculine

BIOLOGICAL SEX

Female-ness

Male-ness

ROMANTICALLY ATTRACTED TO

Women/Females/Femininity

Men/Males/Masculinity

SEXUALLY ATTRACTED TO

Women/Females/Femininity

Men/Males/Masculinity

Gender neutral can identify a person who does not relate to traditional concepts of gender, or someone who sees themselves as without gender.

LGBT+ is an acronym for 'Lesbian, Gay, Bisexual, Transgender plus', describing sexual orientation and gender identities outside of cisgender and heterosexual identities; the + seeks to include other identities that fall under the 'queer' umbrella.

Non-binary is an overall term for gender identities that are not exclusively male or female. A **non-binary person** may identify as a combination of male and female, or neither, or between/beyond genders.

Pansexual is a term that describes romantic, sexual or emotional attraction towards people regardless of their sex or gender identity.

Queer is often used as an umbrella term referring to anyone who is not straight and not cisgender.[11] Historically it was meant as a slur against LGBT+ people, but in recent years it has been reclaimed by LGBT+ communities. However, some LGBT+ people still find the term offensive. 'Queer' is also often used as a broad rejection of labels. In this context, this could be a rejection of any type of label, but most often refers to a rejection of labels for gender and sexual orientation.

Transitioning refers to the process of beginning to live as the gender to which a person identifies, potentially including social, physical and legal changes; not all trans people transition and one does not need to transition in order to live as one's true gender.

Transgender/trans refers to people whose gender identity and expression differ from the sex they were assigned at birth, though not everyone categorized this way considers themselves to be transgender.

If you're meeting many of these terms for the first time, don't be overwhelmed. It's OK to want more information, to feel uncertain, to wonder where this is all leading.

WANT TO KNOW MORE?

Visit our Further Resources section on page 240 for links to sites and publications that explore the rapidly changing LGBT+ landscape.

POSITIVE ACTION

BANK OF AMERICA'S ALLIES PROGRAM LINKS COMING OUT TO PRODUCTIVITY

When we began working with the Bank of America, the company identified the problem of LGBT+ colleagues not feeling safe about coming out at work as the productivity lost in covering up your personal life in day-to-day conversation. The company developed an online Navigator tool, enabling colleagues to make their LGBT+ Ally status visible to the entire organization with a single click. The platform then tracks data related to their engagement with Ally training modules, the LGBT+ network, events and active Allyship, enabling participants to enhance their Ally rating on the platform from bronze to platinum. Incentivizing participation through gamification in this way, the campaign has enlisted over 23,000 Allies globally since launch.

BURBERRY CEO CELEBRATES THE QUEER COMMUNITY FOR LAST COLLECTION

In February 2018, the then CEO of Burberry, Christopher Bailey, dedicated his final collection to the LGBT+ community and included the rainbow throughout his designs. The fashion house unveiled what it called #therainbowcheck – a twist on its signature pattern. Bailey also made generous donations to three charities working with LGBT+ communities around the world. Suki advised the business on which charities to support and was lucky enough to attend the gloriously colorful and emotional show itself. Burberry's clothes are sold in countries where being LGBT+ is a crime. Given the brand's phenomenal reach and influence, Bailey overlooked commercial implications and backed the community. He is also the only openly LGBT+ CEO in the FTSE 100 to date that we've ever known and we adore him for his authenticity and support of the next generation of diverse talent. Suki may also have bought a few items from the collection – they are investment pieces, after all![12]

If you feel concerned that you may now be labeled 'cisgender' for the first time in your life, hold onto that thought. It's all part of the learning curve. Nobody is telling you how to feel about what you're discovering, just that you remain open to all that's new to you. The more you use this language the more we normalize it, which has to be a good thing.

A LEADER TALKS ABOUT SHAPING A WORKPLACE TO INCLUDE LGBT+ COLLEAGUES

RICHARD BRANSON, FOUNDER, VIRGIN GROUP

For me, this journey goes back all the way to 1967, when we set up a charity in London called the Student Advisory Centre. Our idea was to help young people who were struggling with all sorts of issues, from mental health to reproductive choices and rights.

Quite a few of the people who came to the centre felt they had no place to discuss their sexual orientation; many had no one to come out to. They felt rejected by their families, by their communities. Mind you, 1967 was the year Parliament – against a lot of resistance – passed the Sexual Offences Act, which decriminalized some same-sex relations in England and Wales. But much of society remained hostile to gay people, so we wanted to provide support and just let people know that there's nothing wrong with being who you are and loving who you love. We tried to create a bit of a safe haven during what was still a very conservative era. That's when I realized that supporting LGBT+ rights is everybody's business.

This is about happiness, fulfillment, being able to realize your full potential as a human being. My goal in business has always been to make people's lives better, to go beyond the ordinary, to disrupt entrenched systems and to challenge orthodoxy. And that applies as much to the way we treat our own people and the culture we create in the workplace as it applies to the customer experience and the quality of service we provide. If you can't be who you are in the one place where you spend most of your day, something is terribly wrong. So we set out to change that.

We initially started off like many others – without much of a strategy or a detailed plan, just the idea that who you are is something worth protecting, embracing and celebrating. And we've applied that to many of our early ventures, from the music business to aviation and beyond. I think it has made Virgin the employer of choice for some of the most talented, innovative and creative people I've ever met, and when diversity and inclusion becomes part of your DNA, it also becomes a major driver of success. I don't doubt for a second that our early embrace of the issue has helped build Virgin into the global brand we are today.

Of course, over time our business grew, societies began to open up, marriage equality – unthinkable in the 1960s – is now the law of the land in so many places. Consequently, our businesses have begun putting much more structure and policy behind diversity and inclusion, from recruitment to company culture. We are proud of our LGBT+ colleagues. We are proud of how they've helped shape who we are as a business. It's become a real differentiator for our brand.

What always stands out to me is how much our LGBT+ employees, and their Allies, identify with Virgin and what it stands for. There are so many who have said that Virgin has become their family, their support system. That's heartening to hear, especially knowing that many have struggled with their sexuality in other areas of their lives. It tells me that we are not just an ordinary employer.

Well, fortunately there are more openly LGBT+ business leaders – men and women – now than at any other point in the past, and I think their visibility and advocacy have done wonders to build more inclusive workplaces. But quite a bit remains to be done. The most important point is that a commitment to diversity and inclusion has now become material to long-term success. I really believe that. Embracing LGBT+ diversity just says so much about how you run your business, about the talent you seek to attract and retain, and about the ways in which you manage social change. I've always believed it's the right thing to do, but that moral case now goes hand in hand with a very compelling business case.

Sir Richard Branson founded Virgin, one of the world's most admired brands, which has expanded into many diverse sectors, from travel to telecommunications, health to banking and music to leisure. There are now more than 40 Virgin companies worldwide in over 35 countries.

Pronoun Exercise

Try this exercise with a colleague . . .

• Pair up in twos and have one person talk about their weekend while the other interrogates them about their weekend.

• The one doing the questioning should take on the role of an overly nosey colleague, asking all kinds of questions and really trying to know everything about what the other person did that weekend.

• Here's the twist: the person describing their weekend cannot use any gendered pronouns (he/her), names of places or names of people.

Debrief

How did you find the conversation? Easy? Flowing? Strained? Difficult?

If you were the person asking questions, you may have felt as though you weren't really getting to know anything about the other person. Whereas the one answering will likely have had a hard time even forming sentences and may have tripped up a few times.

This experience, simulating someone trying not to reveal their sexuality in the workplace, is common for someone in the closet because they don't feel like they can be themselves.

This 'covering' happens for ethnically diverse people, too – covering accents, elements of identity, trying to downplay their 'blackness', for example. Or for straight white men who might not disclose they are the primary carer at home, for fear of being considered weak or effeminate.

Covering affects us all in different ways, which is why you can help by introducing some of the actions in this chapter.

LET'S ALL BE MORE HONEST WITH OURSELVES AND EACH OTHER

How much longer are we going to shrug or sigh when someone mentions the importance of pronouns at work? Is it really going to be that difficult to make the use of pronouns second nature for everyone?

As it's soon going to become commonplace, why not inspire your team and set an example by using this new, non-binary vocabulary yourself? You'll find it's the gateway to helping your colleagues speak out about the concepts, terms and language in use around gender and identity.

All we're trying to do is help everyone be more themselves at work.

There are plenty more DOs than DON'Ts.

You really can get to know your LGBT+ colleagues.

Here are some questions you could be asking in your organization to help implement LGBT+ inclusion:

- Do we have gender-neutral bathrooms?

- Do we have a transitioning-at-work policy for employees or customers? Does the company help towards the expenses for this?

- Do we support customers or employees with documentation for gender recognition?

- What does the wording in our parental leave policies look like? Is it gender inclusive or is it based around 'maternity and paternity' only?

- Do we have partner benefits?

- What is the procedure for supporting and informing colleagues traveling abroad for work (e.g. legal status of LGBT+ persons and their protection in foreign countries)?

Just take courage and show willingness to have conversations around gender identity and sexual orientation, so that employees and clients recognize yours as an inclusive organization.

GET YOUR ACT TOGETHER

Don't directly ask someone if they're LGBT+, as it's incredibly personal and their choice if they want to disclose it to you.

Ask everyone for their preferred pronouns and include pronouns on your corporate email signatures, e.g. he/his.

Be sure not to confuse being LGBT+ with lifestyle choice or sexual preference – both terms imply that LGBT+ persons can be 'fixed'.

Provide safe spaces where staff can ask questions without fear of judgement.

Produce communications guides and trans-inclusive training – ensure staff are familiar with non-binary pronouns and why they are included.

NEXT>>>>>   BUILD BRIDGES
ACROSS GENERATIONS

CHAPTER 6

BUILD BRIDGES ACROSS GENERATIONS

While you've been considering how to be more inclusive on race, gender and LGBT+, there's something else to understand about the employee base in your organization.

You may well have a really broad age range in your business. On the flip side, you could be a start-up consisting entirely of employees from twenty to forty years old. Either way you slice it, you need diversity of age.

For the first time, the workforce is made up of five different generations, all working alongside one another. The Silent Generation, Baby Boomers, Generation X, Millennials and Gen Z are all striving for success around you.

While it's critical that we continue to treat everyone as an individual, it would be remiss of us not to note the trends we see across each of these generations and what we can learn from them. You will no doubt have questions:

Can we really generalize about generations?
What can we learn from each other?
How do we reduce the 'eye roll' and create a culture of respect?

These are great questions and we need to ask them more often. Later in the chapter, we learn about the approach taken by Dow Jones and hear from Andy Briggs, CEO of Phoenix Group. What you may discover could shock you.

One thing's for sure, each group has plenty to offer and brings its own unique challenges and opportunities.

Don't discount yourself here. You too belong to one of these generations. While your team will look to you to build bridges across the age ranges, your own place among them is important for you to think about. Perhaps more than any other subject, intergenerational understanding offers the opportunity for some fun and true empathy – after all, we've all been young and are on the way to becoming older!

So how about providing some examples of how generational cooperation can play out in both positive and negative ways?

Opening up on the fictions and frictions of generational behavior could help you harness energy, leading to some great new ideas from across the age groups.

APPRECIATE THE GENERATIONAL DIVIDE

Although there are four dominant generations in the workplace today, we have included the Silent Generation, as they are still present in the boardroom and at the head of some organizations. We also need to say that the generations we describe are characteristically Western in nature and may not be recognized at all by people in many areas of the world.

Generations: A Quick Reference Guide

THE SILENT GENERATION

1928–45

From Maya Angelou to Bob Marley

Currently: over 75 years old

The earliest members were children of the Great Depression and the Second World War and may have fought in the Korean War. For some, hard times growing up changed to a chance of prosperity through consumerism, through the American dream and peace in Europe. From this generation came the scientists and astronauts who put men on the moon. Later members were among the first 'teenagers' and led the tumult of 'the Sixties' era which questioned everything. Yet, for many, the 'teenage revolution' passed them by and they recall a time when life was simpler and closer to home and people shut up and just got on with it.

BABY BOOMERS

1946–64

From Freddie Mercury to Sandra Bullock

By far the largest and therefore most diverse, with the greatest wealth and most power today, this generation was the first born with expectations of a good life. The first to experience mass TV communication and advertising. The earliest grew up with Elvis and experienced the civil rights movement and Martin

| Currently:
<75 years old | Luther King, women's emancipation, Vietnam and the Cold War, and the Beatles. Among them were the long-hairs and hippies who rejected the American dream as well as those who rejected the hippies and became staunch supporters of populism and nationalism in their later lives. Members of this generation drove awareness of environmental catastrophe and brought anti-authoritarian activism to the mainstream. |

GENERATION X

| 1965–79

From Janet Jackson to Kobe Bryant

Currently:
<55 years old | Many grew up in the hangover of the Sixties, known as the Seventies, when ideas of progression and idealism began to give way to pressures on standards of living and family cohesion. They witnessed and experienced the breakdown of industry and manufacturing, unemployment and constant clashes between haves and have-nots, as well as the superpowers, as the Cold War ended and Islamic fundamentalism began to shake the world. The earliest members of this generation had to sink or swim in the hedonistic Eighties. The last generation before the Internet, many grew up, learned and worked in a world without computers, then had to adapt to a globalized economy. |

GENERATION Y (MILLENNIALS)

1980–94

From Kim
Kardashian to
Justin Bieber

Currently:
<40 years old

For some, growing up in the Eighties meant an early life of prosperity and expectation, as economic markets boomed for parents who could take advantage of this growth era. For others, the continuation of societal breakdown seemed normal. Single-parent families were common. Computers entered the workplace. While older members have been in the workplace for a quarter of a century, later members were the first not to recognize a pre-Internet world. They grew up in the Nineties with the burgeoning development of the World Wide Web. For them, 'normal' is a digital world full of information and entertainment at their fingertips.

GENERATION Z

1995–2011

From Dua
Lipa to
Shawn
Mendes

The latest generation to join the workplace are said to be born to the Internet. All have experienced the shock of recession and seen expectations around lifestyles threatened, if not curtailed, by falling incomes, climate chaos and worldwide pandemic. Although they are savvy with tech and tend to see themselves as more inclusive, 'the sharing generation', they must be questioning the world that has been left to them

Currently:	by earlier generations. Bombarded by digital
<25 years old	information, their knowledge of the world, even at
	a young age, is vastly superior to that of any
	previous generation. It remains to be seen what
	their understanding and application of this
	knowledge will be.

How would you depict these different generations? Differently, probably. We just scrape into the Millennial definition ourselves: 1980 for Suki and 1981 for Felicity – who always reminds Suki that she is a year younger! And if you don't recognize some of the famous names above, perhaps that's down to your age.

Whatever your perspective, the point we're making here is that, at first, it may not be apparent why getting to grips with the differences in behavior between the generations is important for any organization.

The reality is that the so-called 'generation gap' is at the very forefront of business today. Not surprising, given that five generations in the workplace tend to have different ways of adapting to change, communicating and using technical skills. These differences often present as a reaction to the generation that came before them and can quickly appear contrarian if they aren't tackled head-on.

. Millennials/Generation Y people born between 1980 and 1994 are the most numerous in the workplace now and Gen Z are rapidly making their impact. This is an exciting time and we must remember that there is great value in drawing in Gen X and above to offer guidance and life experience.

With any of these generations, it's not so much age that matters, but the values and outlooks that are common in people within these broad age ranges and how these affect change, communication and skills.

As you learn more about your different team members, you'll become more aware of how life stages change behavior. One life stage may see someone fall neatly into their anticipated bucket, while another stage could shift an individual out of an assumed space. As always, we must never discount the individual in our effort to understand the broader group.

That said, we can use statistics to make some broad assumptions: while younger employees tend to be incentivized by new opportunities, it's likely to be compensation that motivates people in their thirties and forties who may have more obligations outside work, such as houses and children.

Taking this further, people nearing the end of their working lives may apply more value to work–life balance and assistance with retirement.

Considering these very different life stages and paths will help you allocate work assignments and decide the best ways to manage, motivate and reward people in your team appropriately. This, in turn, should improve morale and performance and be good for business.

We think it is worth pointing to the fact that many of the differences and conflicts between generations relate to different understandings of and viewpoints on the very topics in this book – race, gender, LGBT+ etc.

Understanding how different generations may respond to

these topics, as a reaction to their generational upbringing, allows communication and initiatives which promote inclusive cultures to be more effective and not exclude certain ages from engaging with the topics. For example, it is very common for young people to have had some education on LGBT+ communities, either at school or through their preferred media. Older generations have often avoided the topic as it was illegal to be LGBT+ during their earlier years, which makes it more 'taboo' and difficult for them to talk about.

COMMUNICATING ACROSS THE GENERATIONS

Think about it – why would we bother to name different generations, if there were no differences between them? After all, as it develops its broad attitudes, each generation can call upon many culturally defining events and motivations.

By all means learn the terminology for each generation, but don't worry too much about it – very few individuals actually self-identify by generation. What's going to be more useful to you and your team is how you reach people with messaging relevant to their stage of life.

You'll get ahead by learning the secrets of those that came before you and harnessing the energy and ideas of those coming up the ladder.

The Dominant Four Generations – Some Differences and Generalizations

	BABY BOOMERS	GENERATION X	MILLENNIALS (Y)	GENERATION Z
LEADERSHIP STYLE	Status	Competence	Achievement	Collaboration
WORK ATTITUDE	What are we doing?	Why are we doing it?	How are we doing it?	Who is doing it?
BUSINESS FOCUS	Experience	Productivity	Contribution	Innovation
WORK PREFERENCE	Individuality	Independence	Team	Relationships
BEST ENVIRONMENT	Practical but personal, 'my space', expecting formality	Functional, fun, positive, flexible, efficient, fast-paced, informal	Collaborative, creative, positive, diverse	High-touch, high-tech, adapted to diversity and inclusion

	BABY BOOMERS	GENERATION X	MILLENNIALS (Y)	GENERATION Z
CAREER DEVELOPMENT	Static: having made their career moves, may be looking for final roles, with more or less responsibility, depending on personality	Proactive: with more degrees and experience, in and out of work, are expecting recognition and upward moves	Seeking: entering the workforce with more experience than any generation, are continually looking for more experience and opportunities	Self-directing: preferring an independent approach to learning and experience at an early stage of career
RESPOND WELL TO	Clear responsibilities, being respected, spending quality time with supervisors, but left to get on with the job	Informality, independence, time to pursue other interests, having fun at work	Team-oriented environment, feeling engaged, working with bright, creative people, being treated respectfully	Multicultural teams in a human working environment, supportive leadership, positive working relationships

	BABY BOOMERS	GENERATION X	MILLENNIALS (Y)	GENERATION Z
POTENTIAL ISSUES	Looking ahead to retirement, may be rigid and change-averse, could over-value experience and have trouble being managed by younger generations	Authority-challenging, rule-rejecting, cynical, questioning of rigid work environments, shorter-term outlook, can lack people skills	Distaste for menial work, need structure and discipline, high expectations, lack of skills for dealing with difficult people	High tech and hyper-connected, spend an average of three hours on their phones daily
HOW TO MANAGE	Hands off, may need feedback, while looking for respect	Look for access to leadership and information	Want continual feedback	Benefiting from self-directed learning platforms

TALK ABOUT LIVED EXPERIENCE

Harvard Business Review reported that a thorough analysis of twenty different studies with nearly 20,000 people revealed small and inconsistent differences in job attitudes when comparing generational groups. Work on age stereotypes looks at the content and impact of beliefs about people from another age group.

People's stereotypes of older workers were largely positive and included words like 'responsible', 'hard-working' and 'mature'. Yet older workers themselves worried that others might see them as 'boring', 'stubborn' and 'grumpy'.

Stereotypes about younger workers were somewhat less positive, however, resulting in more of a range from positive ('enthusiastic') to negative ('inexperienced'). Even so, younger workers believed that others would see them in a more negative manner than they actually did ('unmotivated' and 'irresponsible').

Rightly or wrongly, everyone carries some stereotypes about other generations, including:

Millennials crave instant recognition without doing the work
Baby Boomers don't understand technology
Gen X are independent and dislike being managed
Gen Z are entitled and think they're the CEO already.

Ageism tends to be more prevalent when looking at development opportunities and recruitment – more so even than race and sexual orientation. In the employee surveys we run through INvolve, we often ask questions like: 'Do you feel you have equal access to opportunities? Do you feel that the workplace cares about D&I?' Analyzing the quantitative data, age tends to be the one where we see the most differences in workplace attitudes, more than any other factor (not intersecting with other characteristics).

Since most of us are shaped by our lived experiences, it is important to talk about them more and compare what they have in common. While people with similar life experiences are more inclined to understand each other than those who didn't share those experiences, people at different life stages have more in common than they know.

MUSIC BELONGS TO ALL GENERATIONS

Boomers born in the Forties, Fifties and Sixties may have created and enjoyed much of the pop culture we know and love today, but the ground was prepared by previous generations. The Greatest Generation (1901–27) discovered jazz and TV, then fought the Second World War. The Silent Generation (1928–45) was raised during times of economic depression and war and was defined by its need to find a voice. As well as the first 'teenagers', the Silent Generation included Elvis, the Beatles, Aretha Franklin and Otis Redding, who clearly found theirs. Its less vocal members finally left the workforce in 2010, just before the children of Millennials were born – Generation Alpha – many of whom will enjoy the music just like several generations before them.

STEPS TO HELP YOU MAKE INTERGENERATIONAL PROGRESS

If you can understand that most of the intergenerational conflict that develops at work is related to motivation and communication style, you'll be making great steps forward.

Here are some useful pointers to manage the differences in those areas:

- Observe your colleagues

- Don't dwell on differences

- Move beyond the labels

- Get to know each other as individuals

- Establish a cross-generational affinity group

- Discourage comments such as 'People my age feel like . . .'

- Build collaborative relationships

- Manage both younger and older generations alike

- Help your younger employees make the transition from school to the workplace

- Don't assume older employees don't want access to career or skills development

- Encourage debate and a safe space for new ideas

- Conduct an annual survey of values, preferred communication style and motivations, cross-analyzed by age/generation

- Create opportunities for cross-generational mentoring

- Mix and match project teams

- Don't be afraid to let newer professionals take the lead sometimes

---

WANT TO KNOW MORE?

There's more and more research on the importance of intergenerational cooperation. For this and the stats that go with it, head to our **Further Resources section on page 239.**

GENERATION ALPHA

THE TERM: describing the current youngest generation, born after 2011 and still being born up to 2025, who will be entering the workplace from 2027 to 2041.

WHAT IT IS: coined in 2008 by Australian researcher Mark McCrindle,[1] to describe the children then yet to be born to the Millennial generation.

CORE IDEA: according to intergenerational author Henry Rose Lee, Generation Alpha are 'Millennials on steroids',[2] truly the first generation to grow up with sophisticated digital technology and make it their own.

AIMS: as yet unknown – watch this space.

WHERE IT'S GOING: in keeping with the tendency of scientific naming to use the Greek alphabet, expect Alpha to precede Beta, Gamma, Delta and so on, as the twenty-first century progresses.

POSITIVE ACTION

DOW JONES ADVOCATES FOR INTERGENERATIONAL INCLUSION

When financial publisher Dow Jones asked itself whether it needed an Employee Resource Group for different ages, the concept of Intergenerational Resource Groups began to form within the company. It focused on three pillars: Talent and Culture, Business Growth, and Social Impact. The company began to identify the blockers that prevent effective working between generations. This led to advocating for inclusive working for all generations, a focus on intersectionality, and enhancing programs to support inclusive behaviors, such as Returnship, Internship, Reverse Mentoring and Networking.

GO OFF-SITE AND LISTEN TO THE STORIES

Often, miscommunication between generations stems from a lack of knowledge. We have found that encouraging the conversation can be a valuable tool in bringing groups together.

By way of a practical exercise, it might do you good to get out of your typical routine and shake up some habitual patterns of behavior.

Setting up a designated time to learn more about each other gives employees a chance to find common ground across generational divides. In an environment where we are increasingly remote, you can also try this exercise via break-out rooms on your video-conferencing platform or even with family and friends.

Campfire Stories

A classic activity that inspires storytelling and improves team bonding. Teams gather in a circle and share their workplace experiences. Along the way, they learn things about each other and relive old memories.[3]

Number of participants: six to twenty
Duration: forty-five minutes
Objective: informal training, encourage participants to share, and establish common experiences

How to play
1. Create a set of trigger words/phrases that can kick-start a storytelling session, e.g. 'first day', 'work travel', 'partnership', 'side project' etc. Add them to sticky notes/make a list, if remote.

2. Divide a whiteboard into two sections (Zoom creates this functionality if remote, or you can point your camera to one person who manages the whiteboard!). Post all sticky notes/the list from above on one section of the whiteboard.

3. Ask a participant to pick out one trigger word from the list and use it to share an experience (say, about their first day at the company). Shift that idea to the other side of the whiteboard.

4. As the participant is relating their experience, ask others to jot down words that remind them of similar work-related stories. Add these words to sticky notes/the list and paste them on the whiteboard.

5. Repeat this process until you have a 'wall of words' with interconnected stories.

Debrief

End the exercise with a discussion around storytelling being at the heart of the community experience. It is also how information gets passed on informally. A storytelling session focused on work-related stories can get a large group to loosen up and share their experiences.

A LEADER DISCUSSES THE POWER OF INTERGENERATIONAL COOPERATION

ANDY BRIGGS, GROUP CEO, PHOENIX GROUP

Throughout my career, I have always enjoyed having my thinking challenged. Diversity of thought is essential in reaching the best decisions, to the benefit of our customers and communities. The idea that only one particular group has all the best answers seems incredible to me. Real insight emerges in cultures which truly value diversity, including the wisdom of experience, as a business imperative.

We are not there yet, but as our societies, both in the UK and the wider world, get older these ideas are gaining traction. We should celebrate increased longevity but we urgently need to change how we think about learning, working and saving to provide for a secure longer life.

As CEO of the UK's largest long-term savings and retirement business, my whole purpose is helping customers enjoy a secure retirement at the time of their choosing. But to save for retirement you need to be able to work and that is where age discrimination hits hard.

The evidence shows that, rather than more experienced employees being a drain, they actually improve both team productivity and customer satisfaction. Age diversity, just as with any characteristic, is beneficial.

A person over fifty who becomes unemployed is less likely than someone from any other group to find new work. That difficulty is exacerbated and compounded by discrimination based on sex, disability or ethnicity. Yet age is taboo in the UK; we are truly youth-obsessed, to our detriment.

I vividly remember having these issues powerfully brought home to me: I was visiting a job centre in East London, in my role with Business in the Community, to get a better understanding of age discrimination in employment. What I heard first-hand from older unemployed people struggling to re-enter the workforce shocked me. The over-fifties in that job centre had written themselves off, just as society had, for no reason other than their age and a lack of relevant retraining. That stayed with me.

As a white man in a position of power, I have learned to assume that discrimination, on multiple levels, is implicit in organizations, usually unintentionally. Each one of us in leadership positions has a responsibility to be visible and vocal in championing positive change. We simply have to prioritize taking action.

Phoenix Group is the UK's largest long-term savings and retirement business, with c.14 million customers and £338 billion of assets under administration. Its purpose is helping people secure a life of possibilities.

IT'S A MATTER OF
UNDERSTANDING AND ACCEPTANCE

Of course, it's obvious that business success now depends on all generations in the workplace understanding each other better and learning from each other. Perhaps it's so obvious that we can't see it. Or we can see it, but are reluctant to grapple with it.

True, some intergenerational conflict in the workplace is inevitable. We just need to recognize that much of it is likely to center on communication styles, motivations and attitudes towards technology. Work out how to get through these and we'll find lots of similar stories that foster understanding and cooperation, based on common values that people share across all age ranges.

Organizations of all kinds have been working across generations for . . . generations. But now, more than ever, we're all considering diversity and inclusion in so many different ways. As life expectancy, medical care and, indeed, financial necessity impact the composition of the workforce, people are retiring later and some are even entering the workforce younger (think apprenticeships, internships etc.), meaning more generations are working on the same teams than ever before.

While behavior between colleagues of different ages is just one of these areas you need to manage, you now have the opportunity to demonstrate your understanding of the power of intergenerational inclusion. Individuals can behave differently when they reach new life stages and need to adapt, so, to avoid animosity creeping in, it's important to build intentional cultures that acknowledge and create empathy around these stages.

Generalizing about generations sounds odd, but reflecting on age diversity has its benefits. Age can be a barrier if we let it, or a fantastic social and economic opportunity if we celebrate it. Your task is to encourage the cross-fertilization of knowledge and experience in your team.

GET YOUR ACT TOGETHER

Recognize five generations in the workplace today and get ready to welcome Alphas in the late 2020s, as the last of the Silent Generation retire.

Avoid reinforcing stereotypes by creating single-generation-based employee affinity groups and assuming you already know how to motivate employees who are older or younger.

Conduct regular HR surveys to get a pulse on your employees' demographics and needs, then develop incentive plans that reflect where your employees are in their lives.

Forge partnerships with employees of different ages and encourage them to share their opinions and experiences.

Create mixed-age teams and reverse-mentoring programs that enable experienced workers to interact with and learn from newer and younger employees, ensuring older and experienced employees are also benefiting from mentorship schemes.

NEXT>>>>>   **INVOLVE 100% OF EVERYONE**

CHAPTER 7

INVOLVE 100% OF EVERYONE

If, by now, you think we've been filling your world with tough choices while asking you to change everything in a single day, don't worry: change takes time, but it must be intentional. True inclusion will not happen organically, it will need you to act.

It is important that you take a good look at your personal leverage. Where do you have the power to influence change for others in your company right now? We're looking for 100% inclusion and that is the place to start.

Let's begin by considering where we are today in the workplace. Many people's new-found appreciation for the effectiveness of the remote or more flexible work environment has opened up doors that might previously have been closed.

It's highly likely that you, a straight white male leader, are in the middle of all this. You appreciate the challenges you're facing and are probably wondering who else does. For instance, employees in middle management tend to live in a conflicted area where they face the daily challenge of balancing the tactical with the strategic. While you may acknowledge that a diverse team statistically yields better results, you also know there's now a need for both greater training and closer oversight. If, that is, you are to ensure cohesion among a group of individuals who bring a broad spectrum of talents and motivations to the table.

Although training for awareness can be a quick solution, it's also a vital one. Especially if we're looking to secure inclusion and belonging for ourselves and our peers, while also optimizing business results that will benefit us and those around us.

The prospect of closer oversight may be unappealing for you and intimidating for your reports, but remote working calls for adapting the rules we wrote for performance in a 'turning up' culture. We'll take a look at this in depth in Chapter 8. Here, in Chapter 7, we challenge you to stop thinking in strands. After we've spent several chapters identifying and celebrating difference, that may sound like a paradox. Yet this is where we step up to a higher level of thinking and behaving.

Let's not make the mistake of assuming that the push for equality diminishes competition and what you, personally, have achieved in your career to date. Far from it. Leveling up provides all the reasons why you should want to compete against everyone in future and test yourself in a truly measurable way. Where business meets nirvana is where we identify that being your authentic self gets the best out of everybody and that vulnerability is a strength and not a weakness.

IT'S TIME FOR HUMAN INCLUSION

This book is a simple introduction to diversity and inclusion. We've focused on gender, race, LGBT+ and age, but diversity is way more than all this. Certain demographics have had more airtime, especially gender. The BLM movement has shone a much-needed spotlight on race inequity and brought this to the forefront of hiring and retention strategy.

While we know this might already be daunting and confusing enough, we do need to give you an overview of other protected characteristics in your workplace. We hope you will explore them in more depth beyond this book.

So let's talk about mental health, disability, neurodiversity, religious affiliation, social mobility and family life, as one thing called HUMAN INCLUSION. And that includes you, a straight white man, and the diversity you bring to the workplace.

We want to celebrate differences and make sure you're armed with knowledge on each of these different areas. Although you're not going to take on board everything in this book straightaway, there are lots of other resources you can review to expand your learning.

We live and work in a beautifully intersectional world. It's time to remove the boxes and enable 100% of everyone to compete on a level playing field.

Business is at its best when people are at their best. Let's ensure people can take their whole selves to work and thrive.

**Remove the boxes, include everyone,
appreciate the difference.**

MAKING SPACE FOR MENTAL HEALTH

In the UK, 30% of the workforce have been formally diagnosed with a mental health condition at some point in their lifetime.[1]

The US has similar stats:[2]

- nearly 1 in 5 adults live with a mental illness (51.5 million in 2019)

- 48% of those aged eighteen to twenty-nine experience loneliness

- 79% of LGBT+ people are likely to have experienced poor mental health where work was a cause or a contributing factor.

What are you calling it? Mental health? Emotional wellbeing? Whatever it is, let's facilitate its inclusion in the workplace.

It's OK to not be OK.

Repeat that again. Say it out loud. Say it to your colleagues and your team. The more we destigmatize mental health, the more we all grow and learn from each other's experiences.

Mental health impacts everyone at some stage in their lives, so it's an issue that doesn't discriminate against any demographic. In fact, it affects some demographics significantly more than others.

Mental health and disability form the next frontier for diversity and are likely to create one of the greatest hurdles for those of us who have been trained for many years to keep our work and our home life separate.

We're transitioning from a traditional environment to the workplace of the future. The old perspective of keeping work and life separate no longer stands and this is affecting you in your role.

Most managers and leaders are still straight white men. You're having to step in as first responders to mental health issues, see the signs in others and get comfortable with having the conversation. Not forgetting your ability to monitor your own mental health.

When you can exemplify 'bringing your whole self to work', you'll help those around you become more productive.

While the common contexts for mental distress and ill health are familiar to many of us, it's worthwhile recognizing what some of the early signs might be that lead to them:

EARLY SIGNS	POTENTIAL ISSUES
Finding it hard to make decisions Poor concentration Irritability and short temper	*Money worries?*
Drinking more Low mood	*Relationship problems?*
Easily distracted Worrying more Feeling overwhelmed by things	*Overworked?*
Tiredness and lack of energy	*Physical pain?*

Talking less Avoiding people and social activities	*Depression?*
Talking more or talking very fast Jumping between topics and ideas Finding it difficult to control emotions Aggression	*Loneliness?*

We'd be missing a trick here not talking about the biggest mental health crisis since 2008 – COVID-19. The UK and the US already had an 'epidemic of loneliness' pre-COVID, and the pandemic made it even worse. People were suffering, and marginalized persons more so (think LGBT+ people stuck in unsupportive homes, ethnically diverse communities dying of COVID at higher rates, parents forced to balance care, education and work simultaneously every day).

We realized we needed to be hypersensitive to our people and their needs. As employees and organizations, we had to be brutally honest that COVID represented a realignment of work–life balance. For some, work was no longer the most important thing in their lives. For others, losing their jobs was a tragedy and finding new work an impossibility. Amid political chaos and everyday survival, more pressing matters began to consume most people. Minds were elsewhere and productivity took a hit across many sectors.

Where this leaves us today is that we need to take the pressure off, take our feet off the gas sometimes, allow people to get their lives and wellbeing in order and recognize some days not everyone will be 100%. Doing this regularly avoids some of the major problems down the line: of retention, long-term leave, consistent underperformance, critical mistakes. Ask people how they are feeling, how they are doing, how you can support. Do they have too much work? Do they need any additional help or resources? This is necessary so that they can avoid burnout and be emotionally and physically well in the long term. We discuss this further in Chapter 8.

Your Mental Health Opportunity

You're a business leader. You have the opportunity to step up and make direct changes to the way you think about and tackle mental health issues.

We urge you to get your act together with these steps as we believe that they will have the biggest impact on your organization's capability to support better mental health:

- **Talk about your feelings.** This isn't a sign of weakness and talking about your own feelings will encourage others to do the same.

- **Ask for help if you need it.** We're not superhuman and we can't do everything all the time. If there's an employee assistance program, then make sure it's communicated to everyone so people know it exists.

- **Be an active listener when checking in with colleagues.** What are they telling you? Are there any signs that mental health might be a challenge for them?

- **Keep the conversation going.** Ask simple open questions, avoid imposing your ideas and show empathy and understanding.

- **Find the language.** Here are some useful phrases and questions:

> *I'm really sorry to hear things have been so tough*
> *I'm pleased you've chosen to talk to me about this*
> *How do you feel this has been affecting your work?*
> *Is there any particular kind of support you think might help?*
> *What would you like to see happening from now on?*

ENGAGING WITH DISABILITY

Over 1.3 billion of 7 billion people across the world live with some form of disability.[3]

If you're surprised at that figure, consider the definition of disability you'll find in dictionaries and the web pages of social service organizations:

> a physical or mental condition that limits a person's movements, senses, or activities. *Disorder; condition; dysfunction; affliction; ailment; complaint; illness; malady; disease; disablement; incapacity; infirmity; special needs; defect; learning difficulties; learning disability; handicap; abnormality; impairment.*

But what about the most common disabilities that people have? A simple online search will produce lists, including many or all of the following:

- Psychiatric disabilities – from major depression, bipolar disorder, schizophrenia and anxiety disorders, to post-traumatic stress disorder and OCD

- Traumatic brain injury

- Epilepsy

- HIV/AIDS

- Diabetes

- Chronic fatigue syndrome

- Cystic fibrosis

Statistics from the World Bank Group Disabled Living Foundation tell us that 80% of disabilities are acquired between the ages of eighteen and sixty-four – the workforce age;[4] and, together with their friends and family, this group has a spending power of $8 trillion.[5]

In the UK, disabled people are more than twice as likely to be unemployed as non-disabled people.[6] The Bureau of Labor Statistics cites the same statistic for the US.[7]

This is unacceptable. The world simply cannot afford to ignore disabled people. So let's be aware that disability is slowly but surely gaining more airtime in business. And recognize the importance of understanding the common challenges facing human beings with disabilities.

When you meet a disabled person, you may assume they're OK because they do not explicitly ask for support. That could be down to the fact they're used to just 'getting on' with their life. Similarly, they may know what they need, but are unable to articulate it.

Accept that, as a non-disabled person, your assumptions can sometimes be wrong. What if the person who you see as having a disability does not see themselves as such? They may not even know they have one. It's possible they haven't been diagnosed. Perhaps they know something is not right, but not what it is or how to get support for it. Or they may simply not know what they need.

One thing's for sure, it's never simply what you can see or surmise. If you make the effort to learn more, you may help a person with a disability to feel understood, accepted and validated as a fellow employee and as a unique individual with their own set of skills to add.

Your Disability Opportunity

You will know someone with a disability. It isn't fair that their opportunities are limited. How might you become a better Ally for the disabled community? Your company, like others, is making use of more remote working, so is there any reason why you can't use this as an opportunity to be more inclusive of disabled people, especially those that found commuting to the office a challenge?

As so many disabilities are also invisible, what kind of an environment can you create where someone can be themselves and feel safe disclosing their disability and asking for the support or resources they need?

Here are a few tips to get your act together:

- **Modify your working arrangements.** Are they fit for purpose for someone with a physical disability? Assistive technologies can be implemented, such as screen readers to magnify the screen, voice recognition technology, hearing loop systems or amplified phones.

- **Make sure flexible working or remote working is the norm in the business.** Particularly for those who may not be able to travel to an office.

- **Fill in the training gaps.** Are you equipped with the knowledge to tackle this subject? What training could your company implement that would help? Myth-busting training around disability could be valuable given the bias the disability community experience. Ask for it in your workplace.

- **Make it explicit all the way through.** From recruitment and onboarding through to external communications on your website, can people see what reasonable adjustments and resources your company has in place to support differently abled employees? Even if someone doesn't ask for the information, tell them anyway.

BEFRIENDING NEURODIVERSITY

According to the BBC, about 1 in 7 people have some form of condition linked to neurodiversity. In the US, it appears in 1 in 42 boys and 1 in 189 girls.[8] You may have one. Many people have one and don't realize it. Some grow well into adulthood without being diagnosed with Asperger's syndrome, for example.

In its simplest definition, neurodiversity is the diversity of human brains and minds. The idea of neurodiversity is still new to many people. Unfortunately, it's a subject about which a little knowledge goes a long way towards avoidance and fear. Especially when neurodiversity is defined in relation to conditions such as ADHD, autism, dyspraxia, dyslexia and Tourette's syndrome. People just see problems and not opportunities.

In the UK, the National Autistic Society has recorded only 16% of autistic adults in full-time employment, although a significant majority (77%) of unemployed autistic people say they want to work.[9]

We often think of autism and the fear of difference it engenders. Neurodiversity also stretches to conditions such as OCD and bipolar disorder.

Yet more and more, we're hearing neurodiversity used as a term describing an approach to education and ability that supports the fact that various neurological conditions are the effect of healthy changes in the human genome.

So here's the important thing: neuro-differences are recognized and appreciated as a social category on a par with ethnicity, sexual orientation, gender or disability.

Whether the figures for neurodiversity are 1 in 7 or 1 in 10, it is not hard to imagine the talent we might be missing out on if we ignore it.

In 2020, the European Union faced a shortage of 800,000 IT workers, particularly in strategically important and rapidly expanding areas such as data analytics and IT services implementation, tasks that are well matched with the abilities of some neurodiverse people.[10]

The special gifts that neurodiversity can bring to the workplace are huge. Some of the most progressive tech and consulting firms have already adapted their HR and resourcing functions to accommodate neurodiversity, embracing the possibilities that come from difference.

According to Forbes, in the US, between 2000 and 2018, the percentage of eight-year-olds diagnosed with autism increased 150% and approximately 50,000 neurodiverse children will age out of the system each year.[11]

The likes of SAP, Hewlett Packard Enterprise, Microsoft, Willis Towers Watson, Ford and EY are noting that, while some adjustments may be necessary, neurodiverse people can be incredibly supportive and a huge help to those around them as they work through complex problems.

About 4% of the UK population have ADHD, which affects the ability to control attention, impulses and concentration, and can cause inattention, hyperactivity and impulsiveness. People with ADHD can often be good at completing urgent or physically demanding tasks, pushing on through setbacks and showing a passion for their work.[12]

This is another complex area to tackle and a good guide is to focus on the individual and their specific needs as opposed to making assumptions or adjustments based on knowing they have this or that 'condition'. Most areas of neurodiversity are unique to the person so there really is no 'one-size-fits-all' approach. For example, you can have autism and still cope with or even like a noisy workplace, so assuming quiet is needed can lead to isolation from colleagues and other issues. But as with all the topics we have covered so far, 'difficult' does not mean 'to be avoided'.

Your Neurodiversity Opportunity

How to get your act together for your neurodivergent colleagues and team:

- **Research and provide some suitable neurodiversity training.** So that you and your team can become comfortable about how to talk about neurodiversity.

- **Be aware that some neurodivergent colleagues may have specific requirements.** For instance, particular lighting or quiet to work effectively.

- **Provide mentors for neurodiverse people.** Mentoring can be very powerful, especially through one-on-one support for short time periods, provided either by someone within the employee's own team or from elsewhere in the organization.

- **Ask HR what resources are in place to support neurodiverse employees.** Or ensure that your organization has the resources and reasonable adjustments necessary, especially bearing in mind those with dyslexia or dyspraxia for whom many simple adjustments can be made to improve their quality of work-life.

EMBRACING RELIGIOUS AFFILIATION

Working with colleagues who have religious affiliations reminds us that we are endeavoring to shift behaviors and not beliefs. This really hinges on the overarching theme of 'Tolerance, Understanding and Communication', which can surely benefit everyone in the workplace.

As with neurodiversity, much of our reluctance to engage with religion is down to the fear of difference. Some, it has to be acknowledged, is attributable to anxiety over potential legal cases, given the prevalence of strong and clear statutes in different countries about employers not discriminating against an employee on the grounds of protected characteristics, including religion.

When it comes to religious practice, it is your responsibility as a leader to set the tone and lead by example. If you hope to work effectively with those with religious affiliations, your ability to understand and offer accommodation to individuals to worship without judgement will be critical.

Yet embracing religious affiliation is not as difficult as it first may seem. Your organization should have a set of diversity policies to support you. On matters such as dress codes affected by religion, including scarves and beards, employers can set certain rules as long as they can justify them with a clear business case, or a health and safety risk. But this is to err on the side of the reactive. Why not take positive steps to embrace religious affiliation in the first place?

Your Religious Affiliation Opportunity

There are several simple steps to get your act together to support employees with religious beliefs:

- **Pay attention to religious holidays.** Share a calendar that supports religious diversity at work, possibly enabling the trading of bank holidays for religious ones.

- **Be responsive to routine requests.** These might include praying at work, for which you could designate a suitable space.

- **Make sure work events are inclusive.** Start providing non-alcoholic drinks and a range of labeled foods and be mindful of dietary requirements and off-site locations.

- **Take the time to learn and ask questions.** For example, over recent years we have seen an increase in companies allowing employees to bring their dogs to work, which may be fine for many but could be extremely challenging if you are from a faith that considers dogs unclean.

- **Reinforce the importance of taking a zero-tolerance approach to harassment.** This means towards or from religious employees. You don't have to be a theologist to respect other people's religious beliefs, but taking an interest costs nothing and makes the person feel included.

ENABLING SOCIAL MOBILITY

People in Britain's top jobs are five times more likely to have attended a private school than the general population. Yet, according to the Sutton Trust, if social mobility in the UK increased to the average level in Western Europe, GDP could be roughly 2% higher.[13]

The US, in this instance, actually offers a counterpoint: 89% of Fortune 100 CEOs graduated from non-Ivy League schools, according to research, with just 11% actually attending prestigious Ivy League institutions.[14]

Often ignored as being too general to talk about, social mobility has long been a bias superseding all others. The reality has been and continues to be that access facilitates greater access and lack of access essentially has you held back and hitting the glass ceiling.

In its research paper *When Gender Discrimination Is Not About Gender*,[15] Stanford University tells us that: 'Employers are simply less willing to hire a worker from a group that performs worse on average, even when this group is instead defined by a non-stereotypical characteristic.' This translates into lost opportunities for those who come from a less typical background and businesses failing to tap into a talent pool that can open up new markets and provide innovation that appeals to a far broader landscape. For example: many sales teams are still made up largely of white men with a passion for playing or watching sports. While they may excel at selling to those with similar traits, opening the team to women and those of different heritage could expand a company's sales by appealing to those that its current team could not relate to as effectively.

Your Social Mobility Opportunity

While, on the face of it, social mobility seems a societal issue, you can also get your act together to address this, too:

- **Measure the socio-economic background of your workforce.** Do this in order to spot gaps in applications, progression and retention; track pathways for diversity over time. For instance, one way we measure this is finding out if the candidate was the first in their family to receive a higher education.

- **Develop and establish diverse routes into your workplace.** Through advertising paid internships and work placements; and making best uses of apprenticeships.

- **Find the best, regardless of background.** Put contextual recruitment practices into place; make sure these are open and honest (more on this in Chapter 9).

- **Give all your employees, with no exceptions, equal opportunities to succeed.** Start by monitoring pay gaps; making sure promotion processes are fair; and creating a welcoming culture that clearly embraces diversity.

- **Work with young people to open up their opportunities.** Collaborate with organizations specializing in working with young people; widen your pool by going beyond the local; use the power of equity to offset financial barriers to attending a company open day.

WELCOMING PARENTS AND FAMILY

The dated view of the alpha male who never sees his child is entirely out of keeping with today's world. Let's give men – i.e. you – the freedom to be parents. To make this happen, parenting benefits need to be gender neutral, allowing for families of all shapes and sizes.

The innovation and opportunities that come from being a parent experiencing changing life stages are boundless. Giving parents equal opportunities will show greater empathy and appreciation for their evolving family needs. In return, the business gets better results through closer engagement and retention.

While large corporations may have impressive and wide-ranging benefits for parents, smaller companies may struggle financially to provide suitable parental benefits. So when it comes to supporting parents and family matters in your company, a lot of the decisions are going to fall on you. Making sure that parents remain engaged and productive may well be down to your ingenuity, creativity and flexibility.

Your Opportunities With Parents in Your Team

Have a look at what you're currently doing, then consider the questions below that might help you get your act together for parental support:

- **Can they make it tonight?** You're putting on after-work drinks at the last minute. But what about those with families who have to plan for such things?

- **What happens to a new parent in a fast-paced company?** Parents face different challenges every day. The responsibilities mount by the minute. Could you offer the possibility of working remotely for a few hours every day, or on certain days?

- **Who else can they turn to?** It can't always be you. But does your company offer mentors for peer-to-peer support? Can the company intranet be of any help?

- **If you're a parent yourself, what example are you setting?** Even if your company has a great parent-friendly policy, if you're not using it, will your employees?

- **What plans do you have for their return?** While nobody's expecting a welcome party, it is important to ease fears and uncertainties about returning to work.

- **Where are they at on their parenting journey?** OK, so your company can't offer on-site daycare, but how aware are you about the evolving nature of your employees' families and how their requirements are going to change?

- **Are you making assumptions about their drive?** Just because they're a new parent doesn't mean they're putting work second. Returning mothers may not thank you for overlooking them for that promotion because you were being considerate of their time. Check in by keeping up the communication.

ACKNOWLEDGING STRAIGHT WHITE MEN

Did you think you weren't part of all this workplace diversity? Or somehow we'd left you out? The fact that we're addressing this book to you should show you that you are very much part of including 100% of everyone.

When we ask you to lead with empathy in your workplace, that's because approximately 70% of executives are white men.[16] And white men have been favoring white men (in countries where white is the dominant demographic) for as long as we can remember. If you're still uncomfortable when you read such a sentence, we urge you to go back to the earlier chapters in this book. This isn't intended as a criticism, it's fact.

You personally may not knowingly have excluded people from your friendship group or workplace, but you have almost certainly done so unconsciously. This is human nature. There are parallels here in the great controversy around Black Lives Matter and All Lives Matter. No one is implying that all lives do not matter, but all lives are not being shot down on their daily jog.

Rather than react to developments by defending your position, retreating or being fearful of doing or saying the wrong thing, why not take some of the actions listed above to support those that are different to you? It's a fantastic opportunity to use your position to show your commitment to being part of the change.

Kris Straub/Chainsawsuit

WANT TO KNOW MORE?

You'll find loads of information on websites, publications and organizations covering a wide range of diversity in **Further Resources on page 244.**

A LEADER SHARES HIS
EXPERIENCE OF WIDER INCLUSION

DENIS MACHUEL, CEO, SODEXO

Growing up, I was surrounded with people living with disabilities. It made me realize early on that not everyone experiences life the same way and it helped me develop a sense of empathy. As I progressed in my career, I realized that empathy, while necessary to build an understanding, is not equity.

A few years after joining Sodexo, I volunteered to become the executive sponsor of our Global Disability Voice Taskforce. It was a cause that I understood well and felt that, given the services Sodexo provided, we could mobilize our teams even more to provide opportunities for people living with disabilities. I still make a personal commitment to attend the final of our 'All for One' culinary competition, which brings together hundred of teams, matching a person living with disability with our chefs to work on a culinary project over the course of a year. Every year, as I chat with our teams, the main outcome is clear: the true magic is not the culinary performance, it's the frank conversations, the 'eye-opener' moments that made our teams more aware of their own misconceptions and biases that hold people with mental or physical disabilities back.

Shortly after I took on my role as CEO of Sodexo in 2018, I attended the annual in-person meeting of our African American Leadership Forum in the United States. Listening to their personal stories, their fears, their goals, their constant struggles – from simple tasks many of us take for granted such as shopping, to changing the way they talked at work in order to feel welcome – my ignorance struck me: I will never be able to even imagine, to grasp, the full extent of their reality. I will never get what it is to be Black in this world. It was incredibly humbling.

Then in 2019, during our Executive Committee meeting, we conducted an exercise to talk about another reality: the corporate world as experienced by our female colleagues. With *my fellow male colleagues, we stood in silence, listening to the stories we couldn't imagine that had happened to these strong, smart, accomplished women as they pursued their professional life: being passed over, diminished or not considered.*

Those experiences help me realize, once again, the dramatic gap of disablism, racism and sexism, between what is said and what is lived, between empathy and actual equity.

As a CEO, I now invite my teams to create such moments in which they purposefully leave their corporate leader outfit at the door and allow themselves to be vulnerable to the discomfort of hearing the hard truths from the daily grind of life of fellow human beings. It's OK to put yourself and your beliefs in jeopardy. It's OK to not always have the right words. It's OK to feel angry, vulnerable or remorseful.

To drive the changes required to make our world more equitable, we must reconcile our corporate actions and commitments with the everyday reality of our colleagues. Because facing our differences makes the difference.

Sodexo is a quality-of-life services company headquartered in France with over 420,000 employees worldwide and revenues of €19 billion in 2020.

VULNERABILITY IS INCLUDED

You've come this far, perhaps only to discover that there's much more to grapple with in diversity and inclusion than you could ever have imagined.

At this stage, it's entirely possible that you're feeling somewhat vulnerable. In which case, you'll be better equipped to empathize with the range of diverse communities you've been exploring. If, however, you can begin to see your vulnerability as a mark of strength, not weakness, what a fantastic position you're already in.

All around you, people will be inspired and motivated because they see you acknowledging your difference in the workplace, whether by being a working parent, living with an invisible disability or suffering from bouts of mental health challenges and sharing this experience. They'll recognize that you, too, genuinely want to support everyone to be their authentic self at work.

Who knows where you can take this power of positivity? Well, we've got some ideas on that for you in Chapters 9 and 10.

As disabilities are both visible and invisible, create an environment where people feel empowered to be themselves and feel safe disclosing their disability or asking for help if they need it.

Educate yourself about neurodiversity, be aware of the breadth of needs each individual may have and avoid generalizing.

Mentor those that may be struggling and be sure that you know what resources your organization provides to support diverse colleagues.

Ensure your recruiting practices are inclusive for all, embrace social mobility and avoid blanketing all roles with a need for a graduate education.

Don't forget your straight white male colleagues and employees, as you need them to understand why diversity, equity and inclusion are as beneficial to them and the business as they are to diverse communities themselves.

NEXT>>>>>   STAY INCLUSIVE AT A DISTANCE

CHAPTER 8

STAY INCLUSIVE AT A DISTANCE

'I'm out to my colleagues at work, but I live with my parents, who are very Catholic and don't know I'm a lesbian. Pride will not be a celebration for me this year.'

'I started in my new role working from home and I barely know anyone I can connect with. I definitely struggle to find my place in my team.'

'It is hard to find a space to work quietly in my house; I live with my mother, my sister and her two children. I feel like I need to hide to have work VCs, otherwise I'm constantly disrupted.'

'I tend to be more of an introvert, and I find it really difficult to participate in team meetings via VC. People think I'm not engaged, I just don't like talking over others.'

Over recent years, particularly since the 2008 recession, many organizations have been building flexibility into their structure. The original motivation was often to make work more accessible for all. The 2020 pandemic forced most organizations to leap forward, all non-essential workers in key cosmopolitan centers went remote and 'the workplace of the future' became today.

The remote working environment we had before the COVID

pandemic was a very different experience to what we've come to know since. So we shouldn't be surprised that, while rapid contingency operations took place as companies adapted to social-distancing measures and the evolution of the crisis, the possibilities and pitfalls of remote working are still being experienced the world over.

If you are able-bodied and work to your own schedule, relatively unencumbered by dependents, remote and flexible working can feel a little disruptive. For some, however, it is the difference between being employed or not.

If you're responsible for children or care of the elderly, you will undoubtedly require more flexibility than others, even if you have some form of childcare or other support. Dependent care has historically often been the domain of women, so remote and flexible working can be a game-changer for women, parents and carers.

The disabled community has also seen a silver lining in the move towards a more remote workplace. Wendi Safstrom makes a good point about this in her role as executive director of the Society for Human Resource Management (SHRM), which supports HR professionals to help make the workforce more inclusive. 'People with disabilities are our most-practiced innovators, they spend most of every day solving problems, removing barriers and inventing ways of doing things . . . With the success of remote work thus far, it's likely that there will be increased opportunities for individuals with disabilities.'[1]

According to SHRM research about the small-business community, 82% of businesses are adopting a broader, more flexible work-from-home policy for all employees.[2] Which could assist people with disabilities looking for remote work as a reasonable accommodation.

Since we're focusing on diversity and inclusion in remote working, we're going to walk you through the importance of keeping an inclusive environment virtually, while you consider its impact on your company's culture. If a virtual environment is new to you, you'll come across the words of wisdom of Keith Barr later in the chapter. CEO of InterContinental Hotels Group plc (IHG), he'll tell you what it's like to manage people across nearly 6,000 hotels in more than a hundred countries.

While many organizations have made big strides towards a more flexible workplace over the past five years, it's entirely possible that none of your team was working remotely before 2020. If so, then the guidance here will be even more useful to you, enabling you to create opportunities by showing a real commitment to diversity and inclusion in new ways.

THE LANGUAGE OF FARAWAY

A new vocabulary is developing around remote working.[3] Perhaps you've established some of it yourself in your organization. Some of the terms regularly associated with remote working include:

Co-located: employees working in the same physical space
Satellite: two or more people or teams working in different offices
Fully distributed: all employees working remotely, from individual locations

Hybrid: some employees are co-located, others are remote
VCs: virtual communications with people who work remotely.

While working remotely provides certain advantages and can save costs, working well remotely calls for a special set of skills in both you – the manager – and your team . . .

THE BEST BITS	THE COMMON CHALLENGES
Fewer interruptions from colleagues	Unplugging from work
Reduced stress from commuting	Loneliness
Minimal office politics	Not feeling listened to
Quieter noise levels	Collaboration and communication
More-comfortable clothes	Distractions at home
Less-frequent meetings	Staying motivated
More-efficient meetings	Taking vacation time
Happier pets	Time management and prioritization
Your rules	Discipline

UNDERSTANDING WHAT'S CHANGING

Should we be surprised that those with experience in working remotely tend to say that it feels somewhat . . . remote?

You're wondering what everyone else is doing. Who are you going to talk to, apart from your pet? Got no pet? Bet you wish you did now!

What did she really mean by that email comment? You can't necessarily reach her, so that you can listen for it in her voice. There's a taste of isolation here, of connection becoming disconnection.

Anyway, what will your manager be thinking about you and your performance? And how come everything is taking longer when we're all connected electronically? Welcome to the delayed-feedback loops of work done by people on the same project at different times.

How do you unplug after work? Bloomberg reported recently that the number of hours being worked has actually increased since March 2020.[4]

Whether you experienced a remote-working honeymoon period or faced challenges from day one, what are you going to put in place to ensure that you remain productive, while still taking time for yourself?

If you and your team get good at this, you'll be developing skills that will transfer to whatever form of work we all eventually settle into. You'll have learned new ways of communicating and collaborating, and how to manage yourself and your time more independently.

WHAT ARE YOU DOING FOR YOUR REMOTE WORKERS?

Some people see the pitfalls and others recognize huge benefits from the increased acceptance of remote working as a viable construct. Whatever the viewpoint, we need to take all into account as we look to make inclusion a priority whether we are remote or face-to-face.

Distance reinforces people's tendency to favor others who are similar to them. It also eliminates the opportunity for spontaneous conversations between different people who may be nearby or passing through.

As diverse communities already experience disparities when compared to the general population, remote working can exacerbate these. As a result, employees may have an increased need to take time off work to care for themselves, partners or loved ones.

Have you had to make accommodations for yourself or for people in your teams? If so, how did you handle this?

When you add your own examples to some of those we've all seen on the Internet – such as the video of the man being interviewed on the BBC when his child comes dancing in through the door – you begin to think about the impact of these cumulative challenges on a wider scale on your organization's culture. You appreciate how operating a remote workforce also creates a set of new challenges, including developing and maintaining a company culture, building relationships and making sure all employees are equally heard.

We're not asking you to second-guess any of this. So we're adding our experience of working inclusively and remotely. The rest of this chapter is devoted to suggesting ways you can make this work in your situation.

PEOPLE NEED PERSONAL COMMUNICATION AND FLEXIBLE MANAGEMENT FOR INDIVIDUAL WELLBEING

Everyone manages change in different ways. Even our individual approaches can alter as we enter another life stage, including how we like to work, and the assumptions we make about others and they make about us. The more questions we ask, the more empathy we're likely to feel.

Sometimes we need support for our wellbeing. Many specialist institutions exist to promote and champion mental health in society. Social justice movements, such as Black Lives Matter, have encouraged people to think about how they manage their emotional wellbeing.

If you lead a team, you can start supporting wellbeing by talking to your colleagues about mental health and wellness, by making it part of your regular conversations about work projects and delivery.

It may feel uncomfortable to begin with, but it's better to include wellbeing as part of the discussion than to avoid it altogether. Remind yourself and your team that we all have biases and we can all make mistakes, but it's important to talk and ask questions of one another. Especially with remote working.

Here are some tips on communication and management as they relate to the wellbeing of your people when remote working.

Personal Communication

- Make it personal – making the effort to know your colleagues on a more personal level creates connectedness within the team and can increase commitment to the overall organization

- Identify and remember their birthdays, the names of their partners and children

- Suggest and commit to having regular informal touchpoints or social activities across teams – some teams might have other ways of engaging that can resonate with your own team

- Try your best to reach out to others outside of the team, and create social opportunities where people exchange thoughts and ideas

- Have a backup plan – as technology may fail, it's crucial to have programs in place to maintain team and company productivity.

Flexible Management

- Make sure you're getting an updated pulse on your team, but limit your assumptions – don't assume you know what employees are thinking, what they're going through or what they need to perform their work

- Ask questions through in-person or virtual one-on-one

conversations, or even an anonymous survey. What do you need from me at this time? What additional resources do you need to perform your job? What is working well? What can be improved upon to enhance the efficiency of our team?

• Offer individuals different forms or levels of support – people come from various socio-economic classes, with different life experiences and caregiving responsibilities

• Remember to include those employees whose roles have been consolidated but are working their notice period – they're very much part of your company and can continue being advocates of your business

• Be prepared to listen when approached by any employee who is struggling.

In a constantly evolving workplace, these are good practices to implement. As you remove barriers for your employees to be able to do their jobs, you'll show you're a leader interested in getting to know the people you work with.

Personalizing Wellbeing in the Workplace

Companies that invest in good, inclusive, up-to-date management training on the importance of wellbeing enable their leaders to create an ongoing personalized mental health plan for individuals in their teams.

Apple, TSB and Twitter are among a raft of high-profile companies to publicly announce and measure their commitment to offering mental health support and increased childcare measures (see Further Resources: Wellbeing in the Workplace, page 244).

Financial PR company the Cicero Group has introduced 'Take II', a flexible working scheme allowing every employee to take two free hours of leave per week. These hours are set aside so that each person can prioritize their mental health, prompting them to use the time as they see fit.

Spotify was the first major tech company to formally launch a 'Work From Anywhere' global policy in February 2021 to fully embrace remote working for all their employees.[5]

YOUR TASK IS TO KEEP IT PRODUCTIVE AND INCLUSIVE

To make sure you include everyone in this form of best practice, you'll need to be aware of how biases that occur face-to-face may well be different in virtual communications with people working remotely.

Some biases – such as physical attributes and gestures – will be less visible. Others will be exaggerated, such as the visual background, audio signals and any technical issues. As not everyone is comfortable with technology, this factor could impact their stress level and, consequently, the impression we get.

VIRTUAL COMMUNICATIONS

CONS

- There's a danger that we will make assumptions about others due to their physical surroundings.

- Without physical interaction, we are also likely to be even more susceptible to biases resulting from verbal cues such as accents, language skills and communication patterns; for instance, the degree our counterpart tends to speak up or keeps silent.

- Even very short technical delays on phone systems can make people assume the responder is unfriendly or distracted.

PROS

- When meeting through screens, we should probably be less worried about biases triggered by physical attributes such as height or weight.

- Similarly, and hopefully, the virtual setting could serve as an equalizer for people with certain physical disabilities; for example, those using a wheelchair.

- No matter where you live, as long as you stay behind a screen you should feel relieved from concerns about possible quick judgements resulting from such physical exchanges as a weak handshake, or using only one hand when exchanging a business card in an Asian culture.

MANAGING BIAS THROUGH
VIRTUAL COMMUNICATIONS

With the increased dependency on video calls, we need to pay more attention to how to manage our biases in this prominent interaction context. Adapting some of the best practices we are already familiar with to the new setting, plus making some other reasonable adjustments, can help ensure we continue to progress in our ability to make objective, unbiased decisions.

The best recommendations we can give you for managing biases in virtual settings are:

1. **Stay concentrated and be mindful.** It's important to remain focused and manage your energy levels. If anything, video calls tend to demand more attention than face-to-face meetings, creating the risk that the extra cognitive load will make us more prone to biased decisions.

   >>> As a first step, do your best to create conducive conditions for making an unbiased decision. Proactively manage your health and wellbeing, avoid multitasking and making decisions when too stressed, rushed, hungry or tired.

2. **Focus on the person, not their background.** While it's natural to be curious about the surroundings behind the person or possible interruptions, it's crucial not to

be swayed by such factors. Zoom in to the person you're speaking with, not the background details behind them.

>>> If you do catch yourself making quick judgements based on such variables, remind yourself that we never really know the reality and challenges the other person is facing now. Where possible, support people to make adjustments, such as changing the background effects, a feature now available in many video platforms.

3. **Keep technology in its place.** Try not to let technology have too big a role. See and use it as a means to connect with others.

>>> If technology causes some difficulties, stay alert to those issues in your assessment of the person you're speaking with. Offer up opportunities for people to contribute in different ways in addition to the video calls.

4. **Continue regular practices.** Carry on following and implementing best practices for mitigating bias. As human beings, we are more likely to spot unconscious bias in others than we are in ourselves, so creating the trusted environment where we can support and challenge each other on our decisions can prove beneficial in mitigating the negative impact of unconscious bias, as well as strengthening our relationships.

>>> When evaluating proposals, have clear decision-making criteria, conduct a structured evaluation process and get perspective from a diverse panel. These practices can help mitigate the impact of biases, whether you meet offline or online.

BUILDING A CULTURE AND ENGAGING EMPLOYEES REMOTELY AREN'T EASY

With less physical contact, everyone has to be more purposeful when communicating. Now that remote working has become so prevalent, we all know the rules for the workplace have been completely rewritten. We recognize you're in the middle of trying to engage and motivate your teams.

We are, too. At Audeliss and INvolve, we implemented a new plan for the working week on Slack. We do 'What's New Mondays', where we share what we did at the weekend or what we're looking forward to for the week ahead. Tuesday to Thursday, a member of the team does a Slack takeover each day, where we discuss hobbies, favorite movies etc., then the member of the team passes the baton to someone else at the end of the day. Finally, we do 'Good News Fridays' to celebrate the successes of the team each week in order to be positive and happy. Slack even has a function where it can randomly pair you with a colleague to have a virtual coffee.

These are super-simple to implement via team/department/business/geography. And they work.

WANT TO KNOW MORE?

According to LifeLabs, managing people at a distance requires the same skillset as managing them in person. With one major difference – 'all of your leadership efforts need to be *much, much more deliberate*'.

For more information about the learning organization's quick tips for managers – including keeping one-on-ones frequent and consistent; creating a 'channel map', advising best use of email, text, phone etc.; designing work that people can do in bursts; and how to lead virtual team meetings effectively – see our **Further Resources section on page 243.**

A LEADER WITH VAST EXPERIENCE OF SUPPORTING COLLEAGUES IN REMOTE PLACES

KEITH BARR, CEO, IHG HOTELS & RESORTS

I've been very fortunate in my career to have worked all over the world in a hospitality industry that is truly all about people. Travel brings different walks of life and cultures together, and time and again I have experienced richer conversations, perspectives and lessons because of it.

As CEO, I've always emphasized how important it is that IHG represents the diversity of those who work for us, stay in our hotels and make up the communities we're a part of. Inclusivity is certainly inherent to true hospitality – but I think also more broadly to any business that wants to encourage innovation, teamwork, loyalty and success.

You will only get so far if you rely on things to happen organically. Inclusivity requires education, transparency, programs and honest conversations. At IHG, we're certainly on our own journey. We welcome and support many different communities, but we've had to focus on increasing female representation among our senior leadership and hotel general managers, and we also recognize a need to be more ethnically diverse.

We've spent a lot of time talking to colleagues, taking in diverse perspectives from around the world and listening to their views about what we can do better. We operate in over a hundred countries, which means we have a huge amount to learn from each other and apply in dealing with different situations.

Our approach has included sessions where we've invited colleagues to give an honest account of their experiences and have some really open conversations around race. This in part led us to make a series of formal commitments in the Americas to support Black colleagues and communities, with a pledge to further increase ethnic representation. Alongside the work we're doing through our global and regional D&I boards, training, partnerships and programs, actions such as these underline inclusivity as being core to what we stand for as an employer and will create meaningful change.

During COVID-19, open, transparent communication with colleagues has been my most valuable tool to ensure everyone feels included. I've always hosted regular calls with senior leaders which work well, and we've added calls to bring together all of our corporate colleagues globally – that's thousands of people from multiple geographies and time zones. These give me the chance to talk about what is happening in the world, the industry, our business and the communities we operate in, and to answer live questions. In the current environment we've used them to deliver important but difficult news, which is key if you want to be transparent with colleagues. Overall, the calls have been really well received as I think people appreciate the candid, honest approach.

We've also thought a lot about groups such as women and ethnic minorities who have been more adversely impacted than others by the pandemic – how can we help by looking at the way we work day to day? We've trained line managers on how to manage colleagues remotely and we've strengthened our flexible working practices to the extent that it's unlikely that we'll ever return to full five-day weeks in the office. Senior leaders are expected to act as role models for work–life balance so that colleagues feel empowered to have the same. During the summer of 2020, we also introduced 'recharge days' on the last Friday of every month to make sure people were getting the chance to switch off their laptops and rest.

Today, people expect companies to take greater responsibility and be much more proactive in contributing to societal change – as a father of two teenage daughters, I can see how this is being driven by the next generation.

Targets have a place, but they must be supported systematically. You need to look closely at your recruitment processes, talent development plans, where you hire from and understand the barriers that are holding you back. If you want to know how to improve as a business, ask your people. While the feedback might not always be what you want to hear, it will be where some of the most important change comes from.

Over time, alongside achieving improved statistics and ratios, it is education and cultural awareness, like addressing unconscious bias, that will represent real long-term success in how we build teams and hire.

IHG Hotels & Resorts is a British multinational hospitality company, with around 6,000 hotels in more than 100 countries. Approximately 350,000 people work across IHG's hotels and corporate offices globally.

YOUR CHANCE TO DEMONSTRATE YOUR COMMITMENT TO INCLUSION

If you can view the dramatic changes in the way we work as an opportunity to build a robust framework for remote-working success, not just as an ongoing problem to solve, you may find that it has benefits which go beyond any crisis, even COVID and its social distancing.

Hopefully, you and your colleagues will be able to call on some help and support from external social networks, family and friends. Many networks are now hosting virtual 'tea and talks' – where members can connect to each other and discuss what is on their mind.

If you're aware of any of these networks supporting discrete communities – from parenting, to ethnicity, to LGBT+ and wellbeing – it's important to ensure they continue to post regularly to their community sites, sharing top tips and information. This way, they are more likely to share what they are hearing from you and your colleagues, so that you can provide further external support and training if needed.

LEAD COMPASSIONATELY

Be open, build the trust, help people feel valued.

If there's one thing highlighted by all the tips and suggestions here, it's that the mental and physical wellbeing of your remote workers is the foundation of remote-working success.

Be clear about everyone's role online.

To establish this, everyone, including management, needs to flex to the unique challenges and opportunities of a remote workforce, including how bias can affect us in different ways virtually.

Forget the quizzes, just get to know each other!

What really shines through, however, is that it's the social element that binds a diverse workforce working remotely. This means taking time out with colleagues over video conferencing or calls – not just to 'get work done', but to socialize. So go on, make that fifteen-minute phone call at the end of the week.

Even if your company does not have the resources, you can lead compassionately. In 2019, US research from Fortune and its partner Great Place to Work explains why the stakes for keeping diversity on top of your organization's agenda are so high.[6] Their study linked D&I and success during an economic downturn: in this instance, the Great Recession. Their data set comprised nearly 4 million employees across a multitude of demographics. They found that diversity and inclusion efforts represent a potent source of strength for organizations as they weather tough times. In particular, the experience of certain groups of employees – including historically disadvantaged ones – predicts whether organizations flatline, survive or thrive during a recession ('thrive' describes publicly held companies in their data set that achieved returns of 14% or greater between 2007 and 2009).

That's the business case that will always be top of mind. Despite this, some companies lack the resources to do more on diversity and inclusion. As a leader who wants to go beyond compliance to deliver really effective inclusion, you may be left wondering what you are going to do.

Well, nothing should stop you leading compassionately, so stop worrying whether people are pulling their weight and start worrying about the weight on their shoulders.

GET YOUR ACT TOGETHER

Embrace remote working – it's here to stay, and the rules are changing fast.

Understand what's changing and begin to address the common challenges, like mental health and wellness and also how to disconnect.

Lead by example, put people first and keep technology in its place.

Learn how to optimize the technology you need to stay connected and don't be afraid to show your vulnerability as you learn new skills.

Check in on your team and colleagues more often, to try and compensate for the lack of physical contact.

NEXT>>>>>   START RECRUITING INCLUSIVELY

CHAPTER 9

START RECRUITING INCLUSIVELY

We have nearly forty years of combined experience within the recruitment world and have certainly heard our share of extraordinary requests. From clients asking for an 'attractive woman' for a front-of-house role; and minority candidates being penalized for 'junior experience' in reference to roles they had twenty years earlier; to women being rejected for not seeming as 'likable' as the male candidates in the process; or LGBT+ candidates being discarded as 'not a culture fit'.

And this barely scratches the surface . . .

While recruiting inclusively will effect real change, we know that the recruitment process in many companies is not fit enough to make it happen. It can be hard to make change, especially with a million other priorities on your list. If you get inclusive recruitment right, however, you will reap the benefits, so we're asking you to make it a priority.

First take a look at your existing population. Do you have up-and-coming talent internally that you can progress into your role? If so, always ensure that you are not engaging in the benevolent bias we referenced in Chapter 2.

It is often true that diverse talent is prevalent at entry level in administration, operations, customer support and other roles. You can boost your pipeline by understanding who has the potential to progress into an executive career. Try not to assume that folks who did not come in via a management track aren't interested in that opportunity. Weave any internal talent into the same process as your external talent and use the tips we outline here to ensure that assessment is fair and equitable for all.

Recruiting, be that internal or external, is never easy and the ramifications of hiring the wrong candidate are significant. We appreciate that the pressure to just go for someone you know or trust is very tempting. So the first and most important thing to remember here is that inclusive recruitment is not about compromising on the quality of the candidate. It is always about widening the gate, not lowering the bar.

HOW DO YOU GRASP THIS OPPORTUNITY?

Given that your organization's familiarity with recruiting inclusively may be recent, there will be a knowledge gap to cross. While it's up to your leadership to identify whether a greater investment or transformation is needed, it's also up to you to accelerate the sourcing and development of diverse talent.

In this chapter, we discuss how to hire new people using an inclusive perspective, providing them with opportunities and assigning team members to different projects. Since HR and recruiting infrastructures are complex, the suggestions we make here can largely be introduced as an enhancement or a bolt-on to any existing policy in your organization.

Start With Principles and Core Values

Does your organization have a value or principle framework? If so, how ingrained is it in your culture?

If you don't have a framework, then it's worth investing the time to create one. Aligning your job descriptions and assessment criteria to your organization's principles and core values is a great foundation for recruiting inclusively. This way you are assessing against a matrix of skills that measure against technical aptitude and culture and help to ensure bias doesn't sneak in.

A huge barrier for diverse candidates is that they often present differences. Maybe they come from a different academic track or career path than others on the team. Having a clear assessment matrix mapped to your values and principles means that the notion of 'not being a fit' needs to be justified against a set of criteria that calls out historical preference and focuses on actual job/culture needs.

Here are some examples of values that other companies use: Google's mission is 'to organize the world's information and make it universally accessible and useful'.[1] American Express believes that 'serving our communities is not only integral to running a business successfully, it is part of our individual responsibilities as citizens of the world.'[2] One of Audible's 'People Principles' is to 'imagine and invent before they ask',[3] i.e. innovate before the customer asks for it.

Culture can feel a little artificial to some, with so many organizations subscribing to similar principles and changing their values fairly regularly. But building an intentional culture that all existing and future employees understand and can speak to is critical. If you allow a culture to develop organically, then you might allow a negative influence to creep in and, as with all things, prevention is better than cure.

A study by tinypulse.com explores this in more depth. 'Today's workers have so much on their plates. In fact, according to our Employee Engagement report, nearly 70% of employees feel as though they are unable to tackle all of their job responsibilities each week. That's tough enough as it is. Add in a co-worker who's constantly complaining about everything, and managing a workload gets that much more difficult. When negative attitudes infiltrate the workplace, employees become disengaged and less productive. And what does less productivity mean for a business? Less revenue.'[4]

When You're Culture Building

- Encourage the use of tools like employee engagement surveys – they'll tie strategic goals to your values and reinforce the mission consistently over the course of a year

- Establish formal and informal check-ins and calibration points – to help you assess when employees may be becoming overwhelmed or disengaged

- Seek this data proactively, to assess for environment, inclusion and belonging – it will support you in resolving problems and ensure you maintain a positive working environment.

ALIGN PRINCIPLES TO COMPETENCIES

What competencies do you need from the role? Thinking about these should enable you to identify considered, probing questions you can use in assessment. First things first: you will need to go through your role description to identify the competencies and also establish how this role can weave into your value structure.

Crafting the right questions is much easier once you have laid the groundwork. As you want candidates to offer examples and multidimensional responses, behavioral and open-ended questions will be your best approach.

So let's take a minute to explore a few question styles. There are many differing views, but all philosophies agree that how you ask your questions is critical. We believe that behavior-based questions are effective in mitigating bias as they focus on proven experience and more accurately determine the future performance or success of the individual.

While we recommend you adopt the approach that works for you, possibly involving a variety of question styles, trusting your gut or taking the safe route is not going to yield the best results!

Harvard Business Review recommends[5] that you share the questions with the candidate ahead of time, then break your approach down to three core sections that:

1. test for preparation

2. test for critical thinking and tech savviness

3. test for listening and communication skills.

Be thoughtful and adhere to your process. The better prepared your candidates and interviewers are, the better results you will get and the more confident you can feel in your hire.

Interview Questions

THEME	STANDARD QUESTION	BEHAVIORAL-BASED QUESTION	CRITICAL THINKING
LEADERSHIP	What is your leadership style?	Can you tell me about a time when you demonstrated leadership?	How do you monitor the performance of the people that you have to lead?
TEAMWORK	What is your management experience?	Talk about a time when you had to manage someone whose personality was very different from yours.	What are the three most important things needed for effective teamwork in the workplace?
CUSTOMER EXPERIENCE	How do you prioritize your customer?	Tell me about a time you went above and beyond what was expected to please a customer?	You are a customer too. What are the main reasons you choose to shop here?

PREPARATION IS KEY

If you look, you'll find plenty of resources available on the Internet and from others in your organization; we leverage sources like LinkedIn[6] and companies like Amazon[7] will outline their entire process online or offer lots of example questions you can use. Borrow where you can and build your findings into your framework. Keeping interviewers aligned to your approach is going to be important. Most people enter an interview process with previous experience and a methodology that has worked for them in the past. They may be reluctant to change their style.

To ensure alignment and buy-in to the process and deliverables, taking the time for a pre-brief with all your interviewers (we often refer to this team as stakeholders!) is essential. Effective interviewing requires all stakeholders to be on board with your approach. Educate, assign questions, align on expectations for feedback. If you are clear in your commitment and build the right foundations, you can make the changes needed to achieve your goals.

To recap: if you assign specific competencies to each interviewer, you will enhance candidate experience by avoiding duplication and increase your odds of effective selection by covering all areas. As everyone is assessing for different skills, you also encourage focus and avoid conveying bias through your interview team.

A SEVEN-STAGE INCLUSIVE RECRUITMENT PROCESS

If you are hiring staff into your team, then you're making the decision and the process needs to be one you believe in. You are the hiring manager and anyone in recruitment supporting you should be there as a guide to help build the structure and ensure it is effectively executed. Your candidates will thank you for a well-crafted process, as they too will feel confident that they got the role for the right reasons.

1. **Build trust.** The process starts with building trust with your interview team. Everyone engaged in the exercise should understand your business and your priorities for this role. This will help them to be open-minded in assessing great (and hopefully diverse) talent.

2. **Be thoughtful.** The more thought and consideration you are able to put into a safe and collaborative assessment and selection process, the better the outcome will be. If you are looking for different profiles, then the role description and potential candidates will need to be reviewed carefully. You should consider getting the input of three or more key stakeholders who can assess the description for technical and cultural components, as well as inclusive language.

3. **Innovate.** Who is doing this job well in your industry and who isn't? If you don't know, that's OK, but it's worth

doing some digging and perhaps asking your team or peers for their thoughts. For example: 'We are looking for digital marketing expertise and I heard that Google has a new SEO optimization approach for zero-click search. It would be great to ask candidates if they are familiar with that.'[8] This way you can ensure that you are targeting candidates in the companies that are leading the way rather than hoping these folks apply to you!

4. **Actively engage.** Speak with your network to find talent or referrals for the job you are hiring. While this will not necessarily bring in the most diverse talent, it will serve as a benchmark for compensation and perhaps other skills you could be assessing. It is always important to map the market. In addition to your network you should consider asking employee resource groups if they have referrals and seeing if there are any non-profits or networking groups geared towards advancing diverse communities; we have seen success working with groups like the Executive Leadership Council and Chief (among others).

5. **Mitigate bias.** Ensure that you mitigate potential bias in the initial review of applicants or outreach. Expand your brief so that you assess résumés from a range of different academic backgrounds, from those with an Ivy League college degree to those with no academics at all, from different industries, different locations etc. It can be easy to skim applications in seconds but widening

the gate to more candidates will increase diversity. Be careful not to fall into old habits and preferences; especially when it comes to post-interview feedback, make sure this is aligned to the assessment criteria you've agreed upon.

6. **Always stick to your process.** While no two candidates are the same and should be assessed on their individual merits, the assessment framework should be consistent for all. We have found that internal candidates or referrals have historically shot straight to the hiring manager, experiencing far fewer assessment stages than others. As a result, they often present better than those who have gone through the rigor of a formal interview process. All candidates should go through the same process, including the niece of your boss or the friend of your colleague who has been referred for the role.

7. **Expand.** The final point is a principle that should be followed throughout. What were you hoping to achieve when you embarked on this hire? Have you maintained that philosophy of widening the gate rather than lowering the bar? Compromise will rarely have successful results. But being thoughtful about what, beyond technical aptitude, could make your team more effective will differentiate you in a meaningful way as a manager.

PREPARE ALL OF YOUR
CANDIDATES FOR SUCCESS

You're ensuring a level playing field. That's what it's all about. The old approach asked candidates 'Why should I hire you?', putting them into a hostile environment and using a more Darwinian process to see who emerged. This might find you the bravest and possibly most extrovert candidate, but not necessarily the best.

To secure a truly diverse, innovative team that will yield the best results for your business means doing what you can to set up every single candidate for success. Assisting them in preparing the right data for your meeting is a good place to start.

Recommend that all candidates prepare by considering:

The company – suggest they review the 'About us' page on your website; what products you offer; what you stand for over and above that product offering; the company culture; have there been any recent media articles on the business, key leadership changes, new initiatives, opinion/thought pieces?

The people – they should review the leadership team and the individuals they are meeting; they might also search for other articles or anecdotes offering insight into the person they will be speaking to.

The competitive landscape – having a sense of who they believe your organization is competing against for business would be useful; this might involve reading up on and gaining a sense of the broader market they are looking to get into.

Their résumé – they should review their résumé with a critical eye in preparation for discussing their career to date, its movement, motivations and the thread that runs through it; suggest they back up each role outlined with experiential examples that map to the competencies of the role or the values of your organization.

Their values – what drives them? How do their guiding principles align with those of your organization? Encourage them in advance to illustrate their commitment to this path with examples, where possible.

Their story – suggest they share some of their background, as a more personal context will also offer further insight into whether this is the right organization for them as well as the right fit for you.

Their successes – remind them to be prepared to call out their successes, even if it feels uncomfortable; being able to back them up with data or tangible results will have greater impact.

Their challenges – given that self-awareness of how you lift yourself up after a fall is key to understanding your value to a team, recommend they prepare to talk about areas where they have faced a significant challenge or failed to reach a goal; with any evidence of how they mitigated this in later attempts.

The role – this is a pretty big part! Ask them to prepare at least three examples that illustrate the core elements required for the role; these examples should focus on why they would be right for the opportunity and the company.

Their questions – suggest they prepare questions ahead of time, adding that intellectual curiosity about the people, the firm or the opportunity will be a valuable chance to set themselves apart from their peers.

Their appearance – given all they have to think about, notes on the dress code may seem like an unwanted extra; but presenting well to your interviewers, be it in person or on Zoom, is an easy way to put candidates at their ease and keep the focus on what they can do, not where they shop.

PREPARE YOUR INTERVIEWERS FOR ALL CANDIDATES

Beyond what we have shared here, we want you to be really thoughtful about your interview plan and the other stakeholders you loop in.

Think carefully about the interviewer group and ensure you have direct line management (if that's not you), one or two key contacts that this candidate would need to collaborate with to be successful, and a strong brand ambassador for your business who is more objective and can assess for qualitative components like culture and motivations. Ideally, these stakeholders will have interviewed candidates in the past and will be advocates for your team and your organization.

The best advice on inclusive recruitment you can give to your interviewers is probably:

BE CONSISTENT	BE HUMAN	BE OPEN-MINDED
Following the same process for ALL candidates – internal, external or referrals – is how you retain diversity in your pipeline. Select a candidate who is best equipped to be a success both within the role and the company, rather than the candidate that feels like the safest bet on paper.	Exercise respect. Remember, you were once in the interview hot seat yourself. Acknowledge that high-potential candidates, particularly those with a diverse background, may have multiple options and it's up to you as well as them to demonstrate why this is the best career move.	Acknowledge the benefits of inclusion of all perspectives. Be aware of any personal preferences or limited viewpoints. Some examples include hometown, alma mater affiliates or geographical location. If not essential to the job, these should not be assessment criteria.

Expect interviews to involve no more than two of your colleagues at a time and try to ensure that they are no more than a week apart. If scheduling extends beyond this period, be sure to brief the candidate on the delay. Panel interviewers with more than two assessors can be intimidating; they can also lead to the bulk of the talking coming from the interviewers rather than the interviewee.

Where possible, make hiring decisions within twenty-four hours of the debrief, with an offer or rejection conveyed within a week of the stakeholder interviews.

Searching for a role can be a tense experience for anyone. Remember that feeling and try to ensure that you are communicating as openly and honestly as you can!

WANT TO KNOW MORE?

If you'd like to read in depth on Inclusive Recruitment, including the seven-stage process, visit our **Further Resources section on page 239.**

A LEADER GETS ON WITH INCLUSIVE RECRUITMENT

DON KATZ, FOUNDER AND EXECUTIVE CHAIRMAN, AUDIBLE INC.

My mentor Ralph Ellison provided the spiritual and intellectual background to the idea that became Audible twenty-five years ago, and from his work and teaching I continue to draw a belief in the inexhaustible capacity for America to achieve its most important mission of equality. Audible moved to Newark in 2007 to be part of the equitable turnaround of a great American city and improve the lives of people in this majority Black and brown city.

One of the first things we did after making Newark our hometown was welcome amazing Newark high-school students to our family as paid interns – they work side by side with English-majors-turned-business-people and elite technologists and actors, giving us a range you don't see in other corporate cultures. We've hired Newark residents from every ward into our Customer Care team, partnering with community organizations and homeless shelters to identify people who may not have degrees but are smart and gregarious, and we overhauled our onboarding and acculturation efforts to welcome them into what the numbers indicate is the most technically adept, high-performing Customer Care team among consumer tech companies. A cultural mantra of 'unleashing the power of giving people a chance' as a successful company is key to this community-hiring program's success.

We founded a venture capital firm, Newark Venture Partners, that aims to attract start-ups to Newark and has helped support nearly a hundred companies, more than half of which are led by people of color and women. We have tried to use our capacity to elevate creators who have too often been deprived of a public voice as we draw powerful words on Black life through our multimillion-dollar fund for emerging playwrights and through embracing Black and brown creators to tell powerful stories, as our deep repertoire indicates.

I continually remind teams that hiring talented people from across the human spectrum isn't just HR's job; it's on all of us. At its best, Audible is a more interesting, dynamic place to work for *our commitment to inclusive hiring, but by being part of Newark's comeback from decades of structural deprivation by headquartering in this historically challenged American city, we focus on jobs at all levels and job families by design, as we also measure how our efforts create more jobs beyond Audible for the people of Newark. These efforts let recruits and longtime employees alike know what we stand for, as they are true to our published People Principles, which call on us to 'exemplify what a company can mean beyond what it does', and they inspire our days. One of the most powerful ways a company can create opportunities and hope in oft-overlooked communities is to move to the urban core and embrace equality-making as a corporate purpose.*

Audible Inc. is an Amazon.com subsidiary and is the leading creator and provider of premium audio storytelling headquartered in Newark in the USA with over 1,600 employees globally.

INCLUSIVE IN MIND, INCLUSIVE IN ACTION

We can spend a lot of time talking about the importance of creating a structured inclusive recruitment process and setting up a value or principle framework. But it won't happen organically. This has to be intentional and have clear goals, with ramifications for not achieving them.

Be sure to establish a structure and thoroughly brief your interviewing team – they are a critical component in the journey to a diverse pipeline. It's crucial they understand interview best practice and how to deliver it.

You'll know you're getting there when all your candidates are competing on a level playing field and you're seeing more diversity being appointed into the roles.

GET YOUR ACT TOGETHER

Recruiting inclusively is about widening the gate not lowering the bar – say it, repeat it and make sure your colleagues know, too.

Find out which diversity networks, both internally and externally, could be relevant for leveraging recommendations of talent out there.

Be thoughtful about the assessment process and use more behavioral and probing questions.

By all means experiment, but take nothing for granted. Preparation is key, and invest the time to implement the best practice recommended in this chapter.

Successful inclusive recruitment means preparing all your candidates for success as well.

NEXT>>>>> BECOME AN ACCOMPLICE FOR DIVERSITY AND INCLUSION

CHAPTER 10

BECOME AN ACCOMPLICE
FOR DIVERSITY AND INCLUSION

We've come a long way together. From eye-opening awareness to practical action.

Our hope is you've become an Ally for diversity and inclusion. You've taken your courage in your hands, started conversations, asked questions, introduced experimental activities into your work projects, seen some succeed better than others. You've been a really useful and supportive mentor to your work colleagues. You've tried. You've learned by doing. You're noting some of the benefits.

That's good, because we're now asking you whether you're ready to take your biggest step yet. One that will surely test your commitment to the cause of diversity and inclusion in the workplace.

Can you now see yourself stepping up from being an Ally to an Accomplice?

What might this mean for me?
What difference will this make to my team?
How will I be perceived in the organization?

If you've reached out, beyond your comfort zone, and been active in taking the lead on inclusion, you may be wondering what else you might possibly do. You could step up and become an Accomplice.

But first, what is an Ally?

An Ally is someone who supports those different to themselves in a positive way. A man can be an Ally to women, a straight person of color can be an Ally to the LGBT+ community, a gay man can be an Ally to a trans woman. Anyone can be an Ally to anyone. It's about being intentional in your behaviors and actions to benefit someone else.

What is an Accomplice?

An Accomplice is someone who is an active Ally. 'What does this mean?' we hear you say.

An Accomplice isn't doing it for themselves. They're taking action to support the greater good and someone else. It's about what you do. Especially behind closed doors. It's about trying to change the system within which we work.

For example, when you're with your fellow straight white men and you hear someone say something sexist, do you address it or let it slide? When the Orlando shooting happened in 2016, where forty-nine largely LGBT+ people were shot dead, did you put the rainbow flag on your email signature to show your support, or did you pick up the phone and check in on your LGBT+ colleagues and donate to LGBT+ causes?

An Accomplice will put their neck on the line for a marginalized group and join them on their march for their rights.

An Accomplice is putting Allyship into action.

Now let us be clear here, being an Ally is great. You wouldn't have bought this book if you didn't want to learn more and take further action. But being an Accomplice is the key to unlocking and accelerating sustainable change in business.

An Accomplice is about encouraging others to take action, too, in the drive for inclusion. It's about speaking up and showing up.

What About Sponsorship?

One of the best things you can do as an Accomplice is to act as a sponsor for others, not just a mentor. As a leader, it's the difference between being 'proactive' and 'active'. Translated into the workplace realities we've been discussing, it's being 'anti-racist', rather than 'not racist'.

Marginalization comes in all shapes and sizes. At the end of this chapter, Ron O'Hanley, CEO of State Street Corporation, will be telling you all about the role of Allyship in understanding this.

Values are great. We all have them. But it's our behavior that counts. It's a fascinating psychological point that we can change our behavior much more easily than our value set. Yet it's changing our behavior that, ultimately, can shift some of the more socially exclusive values we've lived by.

So we're now asking you to step into that behavior-changing activity that will make all the difference in diversity and inclusion.

We're on the journey with you and want to give you all the support we can to understand what it will take for you to step up and take the lead as an Accomplice, a sponsor of diversity and inclusion in life and in your organization.

To place this into a corporate framework, we most commonly associate the Ally role with mentoring and the Accomplice concept with sponsorship.

> *52% of ethnic minority employees*
> *believe they would have to leave*
> *their current organization to*
> *progress in their careers.*[1]

Doesn't the above statistic shock you? What if you could genuinely help this population succeed in their career? You really can by acting as a sponsor.

What Is the Difference Between a Mentor and a Sponsor?

Ahead of the academic definitions, let's begin with the important news that some of the tips we'll be including here come from influential business leaders, who attribute their success in large part to others who have guided and promoted them on their journey.

It is important, however, to understand the differences between a mentorship and sponsorship. If mentors have mentees, what do sponsors have? The answer is protégés.

A mentorship is a long-term relationship built on supporting the growth and development of the mentee. The mentor becomes a foundation of wisdom, teaching and support, but not someone who observes and advises on specific actions or behavioral changes in daily work.

A **sponsorship** is also a long-term relationship, much like a mentorship. It differs in that a sponsorship requires concrete actions from both sides. Sponsors actively seek out and facilitate career-expanding opportunities for their protégé. In turn, the protégé commits to stepping up and demonstrating value to the organization.

The biggest difference between what mentors and sponsors do is probably that mentors work on a one-on-one basis with their mentees and sponsors advocate for their protégés when the latter are not in the room. Already, you can see the difference in behavior.

Taking this further, where mentors give mentees suggestions on how to expand their network, sponsors actually give protégés their active network connections and even make new connections for them.

Mentors offer support and insight. Sponsors champion and promote.

See Further Resources: Sponsorship on page 243 for links to more information.

Mentorship Alone Is Not Enough for Diversity and Inclusion

Although 85% of women and 81% of multicultural professionals need navigational support to advance in their careers, they receive it less often than Caucasian men.[2]

Presenting a similar statistic in a different way, a 2010 Catalyst study revealed that more women than men have been assigned mentors, yet 15% more men won promotions.[3] The findings indicate that, while having more mentorships did not lead to advancement, having a senior sponsor certainly did, and the volume of men advancing in their career is evidence. Put simply, men have greater access to sponsors and this has yielded them greater career opportunities.

The lesson from this is that barriers to advancement for women and minorities in organizations tend to be structural and rooted in unconscious bias.

The concept of homogeneity tends to take over as we are innately drawn to and trust people we share commonalities with. We like what we know and stick with it.

As a result, we become more likely to extend ourselves and advocate for those people, thus creating an unintentional and insular way of cultivating talent.

The remedy? Purposeful sponsorship. Intentional inclusion.

We can do something about what we call the 'affinity bias' – by providing support to those who fall outside the conventional profile of a leader or an emerging leader.

Sponsorship Must Overcome Barriers

As a symbiosis rooted in enhancing individual relationships, sponsorship has implications that permeate throughout a business culture. At its best, it can enhance working culture in many ways and have a tremendous impact on the organization.

Sponsorship requires:

- a meaningful stance towards intentional inclusion
- willingness to acknowledge unconscious bias
- taking concrete steps to mitigate the harmful effects of this bias
- cultivating diversity, retaining talent and training leaders.

When a well-connected senior leader commits to advocating for someone from an under-represented group, it translates at an organizational level, disrupting the patterns that prevent career advancement for women and minorities.

When we look at how a sponsor ought to be using their own visibility and reputation to support individuals, it's not surprising to find evidence that many who consider themselves to be sponsors are acting more like mentors.

To be a true sponsor, a business person has to be able to provide safe spaces for risk taking. A *Harvard Business Review* study found that only 27% of respondents who identified as a sponsor said they advocated for their protégés and as few as 19% reported providing safe space.[4]

Only 23% of sponsors in the Harvard survey said they look for potential protégés with skills or management styles that they do not have themselves.

In its research, Harvard found evidence of 'mini-me syndrome', whereby sponsors disclosed a tendency to select protégés who reminded them of themselves. As such, 71% of self-identified sponsors held that their protégé shared the same race or gender – thus affecting the number of women and minorities getting sponsored.

Our unconscious and affinity biases determine whose company we seek and those individuals who make us comfortable. As individuals, we tend to seek out those who share our race, gender, upbringing, culture, religion. Moreover, white male leadership self-perpetuates, while diverse talent is kept out of the C-suite.

How to Break the Pattern of Bias for Effective Sponsorship

1. **Prioritize difference.** As you begin to assess potential protégés, consider a unique skillset or distinct personal brand. Select a protégé who brings complementary talents to the table. This opens doors to new networks, widens your capacity to deliver as a sponsor, and contributes a valuable management style to the team.

2. **Understand the full dividends.** As a good sponsor, you're able to build deep trust with your protégé and get honest, unfiltered feedback from them, the 'straight talk' that you need. Moreover, your protégé, along with a leader's commitment to sponsorship, can extend your legacy. Take Steve Howe, former managing director at Ernst & Young, for instance. His unwavering commitment to sponsorship has left a myriad of leaders in place at EY to carry on his approach, which includes promoting sponsorship.[5]

3. **Create symbiosis.** Sponsorship is not only beneficial to the protégé; it can have rewarding benefits for the sponsor, too. Done the right way, sponsorship is a symbiotic relationship where both parties can build lasting legacies.

WHAT DOES GOOD SPONSORSHIP LOOK LIKE?

Many sponsors believe that their job begins and ends with the one-on-one relationships they build with their protégés. This is a false notion.

To help create the conditions that foster upward mobility for women and people of color, sponsors must actively support broader efforts and initiatives at the organizational level.

Here are six active ways to get sponsorship working in your organization:

1. **Ensure** that the pool of people being considered for promotions and key assignments reflects the diversity in the organization.

2. **Promote** executive development workshops and seminars that address gender, sexuality, disability and race-related issues.

3. **Support** in-house networks and associations, including networking groups.

4. **Help** colleagues manage their discomfort with race.

5. **Challenge** implicit rules, such as those that assume that people who weren't fast movers early in their careers will never rise to the executive suites.

6. **Make** it personal – decide why sponsorship matters to you and speak about it in those terms. Having a personal driver can be incredibly powerful – whether you want to drive equality for minorities and women or you want to increase business performance.

When Sponsorships Go Wrong

Q: What if . . . my protégé and I turn out to have nothing in common?

Sponsorship doesn't require you to have any commonalities with your protégé. In fact, the whole point of diverse sponsorship is to ensure you are sponsoring people who aren't like you. Take a good hard look at their performance and ability to deliver and make your decision based on that fact, rather than the similarities you two may or may not hold.

Think about whether this person would make you proud if you gave them a risky assignment. If the answer is yes – proceed to allow your protégé a safe space to take risks, and advocate for them when they've done a superb job. Please remember that your protégé can become part of your work legacy!

Lean into your unconscious and affinity biases and don't allow

them to take over for what could turn out to be a mutually beneficial relationship.

*Q: What if . . . I believe my protégé is confirming some stereo-
types of a minority group?*

Don't make any assumptions about orientation, race or gender
identity – sometimes it's our bias talking.
  Ask yourself these three questions:

Is that true?
Is that always true?
Can I think of a time when that wasn't true?

These questions will give you some clarity around whether
those stereotypes are indeed true of your protégé, or whether
it's your bias getting the best of you.
  Very important: always keep in mind diversity of thought and
the different ways in which people work and learn the best. Your
protégé not reminding you of your younger self isn't necessarily a
bad thing. Lead with empathy and the rest will follow.
  Even if you decide you might not be the right sponsor for the
protégé, there is nothing stopping you from introducing them to
someone else in your network who could sponsor them. As you
know more about them, those insights could inform who might be
better placed to support them. Don't abandon them. Be polite
and kind and help them.

See It From a Diverse Point of View

So far, we've been asking you to consider becoming an Accomplice for diversity and inclusion, stepping up to assume the role of a sponsor in your organization.

How about seeing it from the point of view of a person of color who is looking for a sponsor like you? What might they be thinking? What kind of a relationship would they be seeking?

Perhaps they might approach you, as their manager, looking for a sponsor in a different part of the organization? What advice might you give them?

1. **Emphasize commitment**
   - If you want to move upwards within this organization, you're going to need much more than a strong work ethic and an ability to turn in deliverables.
   - Your performance is key to making yourself a known and respected entity here.
   - Your individual performance and team performance combined are what will get you noticed by the right sponsor.
   - While performance is key, be careful not to sacrifice work–life balance.
   - Think about your monthly networking goals and develop an engagement strategy for potential sponsors based on these.

2. Use the power

- Widening and deepening your pool of potential sponsors is the trick to conquering sponsorship.
- Realize that it's easy to choose a sponsor who shares your own similarities or aspects of your identity.
- Take it a step further and choose someone who is out of your comfort zone.
- The truth is that, when it comes to the career advancement of minorities and women, white men matter.
- Men are some of the most valuable stakeholders in this and other organizations around the world, making your participation in sponsorships crucial to the upward mobility of minorities and women.

3. Adopt a bold approach

- While minorities and women often think that great work will lead a sponsor to take notice and select them from the crowd, asking makes a difference.
- 'A closed mouth doesn't get heard.' If you never ask for a sponsor, you're not likely to get one.
- Once you've made yourself known within the organization, start piecing together a diverse network of sponsors and work towards performing at your best. It's vital that you self-advocate for pay rises, promotions and especially challenging assignments.

It's through relationships that organizational cultures, structures and opportunities become knowable and accessible. Women and minorities need to cultivate these relationships with their white male colleagues, not just those that belong to the same affinity group.

ALLIES AND ACCOMPLICES WORKING TOGETHER

The good collaborator understands the usefulness of mentors but acts on the knowledge that the real key to women and minorities climbing up the corporate ladder is sponsors.

The move from Ally to Accomplice sounds like a big one, but we've highlighted some small and simple ways to be a good sponsor and to get noticed by one.

Sponsoring others to climb the corporate ladder is something to work at and master. Do it by becoming the best sponsor you can be today and you'll leave a legacy of future sponsorship for others to follow.

So, we've mentioned educating yourself more than once in the book. You're doing it already by reading this chapter. You now know how to sponsor someone in your company.

What Else Could You Do?

- **Intention.** You don't need to be an expert to be an advocate, it's all about intention. If you make a mistake, apologize and correct yourself.

- **Impact.** Sometimes good intentions can still have negative impact – open yourself up to feedback and humility.

- **Community.** You don't need to belong to a certain community to advocate for that community.

- **Learning.** Watch, listen and read. The space of inclusion is constantly evolving, so educating yourself is key. It's not a 'one and done' scenario, and there are many different perspectives within the space.

What Else Could You Be?

- **Be willing to learn:** develop a passion to learn more
- **Be inclusive:** take small and subtle steps towards an inclusive culture
- **Be brave:** feel comfortable calling out negative language and behavior
- **Be visible:** consciously and visibly commit to inclusion.

Alternatively, you could just listen to ABBA (a big thank you to Ryan Vincent in our INvolve team for creating this!):

- **Advocate:** by showing up and speaking out about diversity and inclusion
- **Be humble:** admit when you don't know something or have made a mistake, apologize and open yourself up to learning

- **Be respectful:** respect how someone identifies, what pronouns they use and their privacy

- **Assume nothing:** never assume anything about someone else's identity or experiences. Listen and learn first when unsure.

In summary:

An *Ally/mentor*:
- *educates themselves on diversity and inclusion*

- *monitors their own behaviors and mitigates their own biases*

- *acts privately in support of diverse groups or only within their own circles*

- *advocates within their direct sphere of influence.*

An *Accomplice/sponsor*:
- *educates others on diversity and inclusion*

- *calls out negative behaviors in others*

- *advocates publicly in support of diverse groups*

- *shows up when it matters: events, initiatives, programs*

- *empathizes with and supports minority groups during trying times*

- *participates actively*

- *makes space for and lifts up diverse voices/groups*

- *sponsors diverse talent actively*

- *questions processes and practices for bias.*

NOW YOU'VE COME THIS FAR . . . A FEW FINAL THOUGHTS

It's Time to Own Your Privilege and Feel the Pain

This is asking a lot of you, but it is the best way forward. It's hard, because it means confronting the possibility that your success may be partly owed to those privileges and opportunities others have not had access to, and that you entered the playing field with an advantage over others.

It's Time to Hear the Feedback and Accept It

Now you're aware of the power games taking place and who is likely to be on the losing side, you personally have nothing to lose when you hear stuff that's difficult to hear about people's experiences in the workplace. If you show you believe what you're hearing, you're in a great position to do the work that needs doing. Don't go on the defensive when someone calls you out for a micro-aggression or bias either: lead by example and listen and understand.

It's Time to Stand Up and Say It

More often than before, you're going to need to be more vigilant in your workplace. You know more. You understand more. You can see the subtle microaggressions and note the minor manipulations. You're going to have to intervene and say it when you see it. Don't 'cancel' others, lead with empathy and vulnerability and others will follow.

It's Time to Build a Community and Push for Organizational Change

When you become an Ally, you learn to recognize others like you in the organization. Now you can build a community of Allies. The more people who understand the need for change, the more credibility and influence you can have together inside your organization. The truth is that members of under-represented groups in your workplace need powerful white male Allies and Accomplices to lead this change.

The time is now.

WANT TO KNOW MORE?

You'll find further reading and exploration opportunities on the subject of inclusive sponsorship, advocates and Allies in our **Further Resources section on page 243.**

A LEADER EXTOLS
THE VIRTUES OF ALLYSHIP

RON O'HANLEY, CHAIRMAN AND CEO, STATE STREET CORPORATION

Allyship has been crucial in helping majority groups understand how the marginalization or oppression of minority groups fundamentally demeans their own humanity. That is the first step towards collective ownership of breaking down the systemic barriers to equality across the board. Whether it is the men who join the #MeToo movement or white marchers who join the #BlackLivesMatter protests, or the mothers and fathers of gay children who fight for their equal rights, we need to lift our collective voices and reaffirm Martin Luther King's truth that we are 'tied in a single garment of destiny'. Injustice anywhere is, indeed, a threat to justice everywhere.

Marginalization comes in all shapes and sizes. Early in my career as a management consultant, I experienced the arrival at the firm of a young woman who did not 'fit' the stereotypical social and cultural pedigree of the majority of the firm's professionals. She was perceived by many as being 'rough around the edges' and did not comport herself according to the usual firm norms. Yet she was also a fabulous thinker and problem solver. I was her first project manager and saw her extraordinary talents first-hand. Yet senior partners at the firm viewed her as a 'hiring mistake' and wanted to move on. I made my case and she was given more time. In the end she rose to the highest levels of the firm, but not before she had overcome countless prejudices based on superficial qualities that blinded so many to her true talents. I often think of her example when I discuss unconscious bias with my leadership team as we consider diverse candidates.

Allyship helps us uncover those unconscious biases. To me, it is about listening, learning and leaning into inclusion. As a leader, it's also about cultivating empathy, humility and compassion, traits that white men of my generation were not necessarily trained to develop. When State Street launched the Fearless Girl statue on Wall Street to promote gender diversity on corporate boards, I was humbled by how powerful that symbol became overnight. It so clearly struck a thunderous chord with women of all ages and backgrounds around the world. One small girl looking resolutely to a future in which gender no longer defines opportunity. Such a simple idea, so difficult to achieve. Gender, race, religion, ethnicity, sexual orientation – fearless Allies in business and beyond need to step up and link their fate to the fate of every marginalized group whose oppression keeps us all back.

State Street Corporation is one of the world's largest servicers and managers of institutional assets, with revenues of close to $12 billion and 40,000 employees. State Street's purpose is to help achieve better outcomes for the world's investors and the people they serve.

GET YOUR ACT TOGETHER

Show up and actively participate in diversity networks in your business – live it with your diverse colleagues and don't just wear the badge.

Encourage your straight white male colleagues to get involved and support minorities in the business, simply by asking them to read this book or add their pronouns to their email signature.

Becoming an Accomplice by sponsoring others is the best thing you can do for inclusion, so find a protégé and get to work.

Call out any prejudice or microaggressions and stand up for the person on the receiving end – you will be an advocate for positive cultural and organizational change in the business.

Commit to reading one of the resources we recommend in this book and continue your learning.

NEXT>>>>>   CONCLUSION

CONCLUSION

Congratulations – you've reached the end of this guide.

How was it for you?

While we know there's a lot to take in, we hope we've provided you with some tools and knowledge that you can take back to your workplace.

We want you to be Accomplices for diversity and inclusion.

We want you to drive this movement of change to get your act together. This means you specifically, but also for you to ACT TOGETHER with your straight white male colleagues.

You can do it alone, but you'll only get so far. Imagine how much more you could achieve if you brought others along on this journey.

We've shown you that diverse communities would benefit from your support. You represent 70% of the workforce. We need you on our side to create a fairer and more inclusive culture in business. You've got this. We believe in you.

We've tried to keep our messages as simple as possible, but even if you don't follow them all, we beg you to take these ten actions when you put this book down:

1. Accept that there is a clear business case for inclusion.

2. Interrogate your own biases and preferences and be honest about them – take the Harvard test.

3. Educate yourself about race and racism, starting with the history of your own country.

4. Make sure that women have a seat at the table and are heard.

5. Signal your new LGBT+ inclusive ways by adding your pronouns onto your email signature.

6. Don't assume you already know how to motivate employees who are older or younger.

7. Destigmatize mental health, by sharing your own issues with your colleagues.

8. Check in on your team and colleagues more often, now remote working is a norm.

9. Explore internal and external networks to find a broader range of talent.

10. Sponsor someone different to you in your organization to help them climb the career ladder.

See these action points as your Ten Diversity and Inclusion Principles.

By taking action, you are helping us all live a more fulfilled and satisfied life at work. These are baby steps and we are confident you can do far more.

We'd love to hear your feedback. If you have any questions or want to learn more, you can follow us across many social media platforms and we will try to help you:

Felicity Hassan
Linkedin https://www.linkedin.com/in/felicitybt

Suki Sandhu
Twitter/Instagram @mrsukisandhu
LinkedIn https://www.linkedin.com/in/mrsukisandhu/
Websites www.audeliss.com and www.involvepeople.org

Thanks for joining us on this journey.

Now, go GET YOUR ACT TOGETHER.

FURTHER RESOURCES

REPORTS FOR FURTHER
RESEARCH ON DIVERSITY

Boston Consulting Group: *Fixing the Flawed Approach to Diversity*
https://www.bcg.com/publications/2019/fixing-the-flawed-approach-to-diversity.aspx

—Innovation through Diversity
https://www.bcg.com/publications/2017/people-organization-leadership-talent-innovation-through-diversity-mix-that-matters.aspx

Deloitte: *Eight Powerful Truths About Diversity and Inclusion*
https://www2.deloitte.com/us/en/insights/deloitte-review/issue-22/diversity-and-inclusion-at-work-eight-powerful-truths.html

Gov.uk: *Population of England and Wales. Ethnicity stats. Gender stats*
https://www.ethnicity-facts-figures.service.gov.uk/uk-population-by-ethnicity/national-and-regional-populations/population-of-england-and-wales/latest

Harvard Business Review: *The Other Diversity Dividend*
https://hbr.org/2018/07/the-other-diversity-dividend

INvolve: *The Ethnicity Pay Gap: A Framework for Reporting*
https://cdn.ymaws.com/involve.site-ym.com/resource/collection/
C757E2CB-5546-43FF-BB71-B56AC65CD672/Ethnicity_Pay_
Gap_Reporting_White_Paper.pdf

—LB+ Women
https://cdn.ymaws.com/involve.site-ym.com/resource/collection/
C757E2CB-5546-43FF-BB71-B56AC65CD672/LB_Research_
FINAL.pdf

INvolve and CEBR: *The Value of Diversity*
https://cdn.ymaws.com/involve.site-ym.com/resource/collection/
C757E2CB-5546-43FF-BB71-B56AC65CD672/The_Value_of_
Diversity_Final_-_09.04.18.pdf

McKinsey: *Diversity Wins: How Inclusion Matters*
https://www.mckinsey.com/featured-insights/diversity-and-
inclusion/diversity-wins-how-inclusion-matters#

—Delivering through Diversity
https://www.mckinsey.com/business-functions/organization/
our-insights/delivering-through-diversity

Parker: *Ethnic Diversity Enriching Business Leadership*
https://assets.ey.com/content/dam/ey-sites/ey-com/en_uk/
news/2020/02/ey-parker-review-2020-report-final.pdf

United States Census Bureau: *Population statistics on states, counties, cities and towns*
https://www.census.gov/quickfacts/fact/table/US/PST045219

A TO Z OF DIVERSITY AND INCLUSION THEMES IN THE BOOK

Bias

If you're interested in a free online bias test, try one from Harvard University: https://implicit.harvard.edu/implicit/takeatest.html

'It is well known that people don't always "speak their minds", and it is suspected that people don't always "know their minds".'

Combining multiple-choice questions and visual cues, these confidential Implicit Association Tests demonstrate conscious–unconscious divergences and support important ongoing scientific psychology research.

Go on, surprise yourself! Do it. Suggest others do it. What a great way to start a conversation!

https://www.shrm.org/resourcesandtools/hr-topics/behavioral-competencies/pages/study-on-bias-reveals-several-types-of-discrimination.aspx

Books
Mahzarin Banaji, *Blindspot: Hidden Biases of Good People* (Bantam, 2016)
Jennifer Eberhardt, *Biased* (Windmill Books, 2020)

Disability

What can you do? The US campaign for disability employment:
https://www.whatcanyoudocampaign.org/about/

https://www.dol.gov/agencies/odep/publications/fact-sheets/
diverse-perspectives-people-with-disabilities-fulfilling-your-
business-goals

https://www.thevaluable500.com/

Equality and Equity

https://social-change.co.uk/blog/2019-03-29-equality-and-
equity#:~:text=The%20Equality%20and%20Human%20
Rights,the%20same%20treatment%20and%20support

https://www.mentalfloss.com/article/625404/equity-vs-equality-
what-is-the-difference#:~:text=Equality%20has%20to%20
do%20with,the%20needs%20of%20the%20recipients

Inclusive Recruitment

https://www.youtube.com/user/OUTstandingiB

Intergenerational

https://www.slalom.com/insights/adapting-multigenerational-
workforce

https://www.shrm.org/hr-today/news/all-things-work/pages/
how-to-avoid-ageism.aspx

LGBT+

Economics of international LGBT+ inclusion internationally: https://open-for-business.org/working-globally-report

Book
Alan Downs, *The Velvet Rage: Overcoming the Pain of Growing Up Gay in a Straight Man's World* (Da Capo Lifelong Books, 2012)

Mental Health

Culture Amp is a 'people and culture' platform that makes it easy to collect, understand and act on employee feedback:

https://www.cultureamp.com/blog/5-ways-to-achieve-mental-health-inclusivity-in-the-workplace/

https://www.forbes.com/sites/onemind/2020/07/14/the-essential-role-of-mental-health-for-a-diverse-inclusive-workplace/#5d7b694aac4d

https://www.cdc.gov/workplacehealthpromotion/tools-resources/workplace-health/mental-health/index.html

Neurodiversity

Understood.org leads with its strapline, 'Shaping the world for difference™'. The organization is dedicated to shaping a world where millions of people who learn and think differently can

thrive at home, at school and at work: https://www.understood.
org/en/friends-feelings/empowering-your-child/building-on-
strengths/neurodiversity-what-you-need-to-know

https://hbr.org/2017/05/neurodiversity-as-a-competitive-
advantage

https://www.peoplemanagement.co.uk/long-reads/articles/
employers-hiring-neurodiversity#_ga=2.8343793.2118190836.
1599653448-472157298.1599653448

Parents and Family

https://medium.com/@peopletech/support-parents-in-the-
workplace-with-these-practical-steps-for-inclusion-
158479be7a83#:~:text=Nurturing%20the%20parents%20in%20
your,higher%20morale%2C%20and%20longer%20retention

https://www.forbes.com/sites/break-the-future/2018/03/28/
how-to-make-the-workplace-work-for-parents-and-everyone-
working-mothers-deepti-kapur/#5a0f7d3e5bba

Race

Black Lives Matter is on a mission to eradicate white supremacy
and build local power to intervene in violence inflicted on Black
communities by the state and vigilantes:
https://blacklivesmatter.com

https://mitsloan.mit.edu/ideas-made-to-matter/a-5-part-
framework-talking-about-racism-work

https://www.pewresearch.org/global/2019/04/22/how-people-around-the-world-view-diversity-in-their-countries/

Books
Akala, *Natives: Race and Class in the Ruins of Empire* (Two Roads, 2019)

Michelle Alexander, *The New Jim Crow: Mass Incarceration in the Age of Colorblindness* (The New Press, 2020)

Patricia Hill Collins, *Black Feminist Thought* (Routledge Classics, 2008)

Robin DiAngelo, *White Fragility: Why It's So Hard for White People to Talk About Racism* (Generic, 2019)

Reni Eddo-Lodge, *Why I'm No Longer Talking to White People About Race* (Bloomsbury, 2020)

Afua Hirsch, *Brit(ish): On Race, Identity and Belonging* (Vintage, 2018)

Ibram X. Kendi, *How to Be an Antiracist* (Penguin, 2020)

Robert Livingston, *The Conversation* (Penguin, 2021)

Audre Lorde, *Sister Outsider* (Penguin, 2019)

Ijeoma Oluo, *So You Want to Talk About Race* (Seal Press, 2020)

Layla F. Saad, *Me and White Supremacy* (Quercus, 2020)

Nikesh Shukla, *The Good Immigrant* (Back Bay Books, 2020)

Religious Affiliation

https://www.hrdive.com/news/google-earns-top-ranking-for-religious-inclusion/571530/

https://study.com/academy/lesson/religious-inclusion-in-the-workplace-definition-benefits-examples.html#:~:text=Being%20inclusive%20of%20religion%20in%20the%20workplace%20means%20respecting%20the,of%20the%20individual's%20religious%20practices

Remote Working

https://explore.cultureamp.com/c/lifelabs-learning-co?x=RqMNYu

Social Mobility

https://www.ebrd.com/what-we-do/projects-and-sectors/economic-inclusion.html

https://www2.deloitte.com/content/dam/Deloitte/my/Documents/risk/my-risk-sdg10-economic-benefits-of-improving-social-inclusion.pdf

https://www.theatlantic.com/politics/archive/2014/01/how-economic-inclusion-can-lead-to-success/430515/

Sponsorship

https://inclusion.slac.stanford.edu/sites/inclusion.slac.stanford.edu/files/The_Key_Role_of_a_Sponsorship_for_Diverse_Talent.pdf https://hrexecutive.com/uncovering-the-true-value-of-sponsorships-in-the-workplace/

Straight White Men

https://hbr.org/2019/10/how-to-show-white-men-that-diversity-and-inclusion-efforts-need-them

https://ndcnews.org/2018/08/30/the-white-male-minefield-how-to-make-diversity-inclusion-more-inclusive/

https://www.forbes.com/sites/janicegassam/2018/09/03/how-to-get-white-men-on-board-with-diversity-and-inclusion-efforts/#4a5e51c17694

https://leanin.org/tips/mvp

Wellbeing in the Workplace

Apple: https://www.imore.com/apple-expands-parental-leave-and-mental-health-benefits-all-its-employees

Cicero: https://cicero-group.com/careers/

TSB: https://engageemployee.com/tsb-extends-mental-health-support-to-friends-and-families-of-staff/

Twitter: https://blog.twitter.com/en_us/topics/company/2020/An-update-on-our-continuity-strategy-during-COVID-19.html

Women

https://www.pnas.org/content/117/13/6990

https://hbr.org/2020/12/why-arent-we-making-more-progress-towards-gender-equity

https://www.worldbank.org/en/news/opinion/2020/04/13/gender-equality-why-it-matters-especially-in-a-time-of-crisis

https://www.un.org/en/sections/issues-depth/gender-equality/

https://www.weforum.org/reports/gender-gap-2020-report-100-years-pay-equality

https://www.catalyst.org/

https://www.c200.org/

https://www.wbcollaborative.org/

http://womenceoreport.org/

https://30percentclub.org/

Books
Emily Chang, *Brotopia* (Portfolio, 2018)

Caroline Criado-Perez, *Invisible Women* (Vintage, 2020)

NOTES

INTRODUCTION

1 Women CEOs in America report (2020).

2 ibid.

3 ibid.

4 https://www.statista.com/statistics/737923/
us-population-by-gender/

5 Business in the Community, UK.

6 https://www.mckinsey.com/~/media/mckinsey/
featured%20insights/diversity%20and%20inclusion/
diversity%20wins%20how%20inclusion%20matters/
diversity-wins-how-inclusion-matters-vf.pdf

7 https://fortune.com/longform/fortune

8 https://www.statista.com/statistics/737923/us-population-
by-gender/

9 McKinsey, op. cit.

10 Race at Work Scorecard report (2018).

11 https://www.hrc.org/news/hrc-report-startling-data-
reveals-half-of-lgbtq-employees-in-us-remain-clos

12 https://www.bls.gov/news.release/disabl.nr0.htm

1. YOU ARE PART OF THE SOLUTION

1 https://www.merriam-webster.com/dictionary/cisgender

2 https://www.thegentlemansjournal.com/greatest-quotes-henry-ford/

3 https://medium.com/@krysburnette/its-2019-and-we-are-still-talking-about-equity-diversity-and-inclusion-dd00c9a66113

4 https://www.merriam-webster.com/dictionary/diversity

5 https://www.lsu.edu/eng/news/2018/03/03-28-18-diversity.php

6 https://builtin.com/diversity-inclusion

7 https://www.collinsdictionary.com/dictionary/english/equity

8 https://culturalorganizing.org/the-problem-with-that-equity-vs-equality-graphic/

9 https://www.vernamyers.com/2017/02/04/diversity-doesnt-stick-without-inclusion/

10 https://www.theguardian.com/society/2018/oct/21/michael-young-and-the-perils-of-meritocracy

11 https://www.merriam-webster.com/dictionary/meritocracy

12 https://www.her.ie/life/new-study-says-less-50-per-cent-teenagers-identify-straight-478613

13 https://www.cjr.org/language_corner/intersectionality.php

14 Accenture (2018). *When She Rises, We All Rise*. Available at: https://www.accenture.com/acnmedia/Accenture/pdf/Accenture-Getting-to-Equal-POV.pdf

15 McKinsey (2020). *Diversity Wins: How Inclusion Matters*. Available at: https://www.mckinsey.com/featured-insights/diversity-and-inclusion/diversity-wins-how-inclusion-matters#

16 https://www.salesforce.com/blog/2017/04/salesforce-equal-pay-assessment-update.html?d=70130000000tP4G%20

17 https://www.businessinsider.com/reddit-cofounder-alexis-ohanian-steps-down-2020-6?r=US&IR=T

18 ibid.

19 https://www.lexico.com/definition/privilege

20 https://www.doctorsoftheworld.org.uk/wp-content/uploads/2018/11/Delays-and-destitution-An-audit-of-Doctors-of-the-Worlds-Hospital-Access-Project-July-2018-20.pdf

2. PUT BIAS IN ITS PLACE

1 https://www.vexplode.com/en/tedx/how-to-outsmart-your-own-unconscious-bias-valerie-alexander-tedxpasadena/

2 https://hbr.org/2017/08/when-employees-think-the-boss-is-unfair-theyre-more-likely-to-disengage-and-leave

3 https://thedecisionlab.com/biases/commitment-bias/

4 https://www.vox.com/culture/2019/8/26/20828559/taylor-swift-kanye-west-2009-mtv-vmas-explained

5 https://www.bbc.co.uk/bbcthree/article/ab1eaf4a-c794-420a-929f-253695ede704

3. LET'S TALK ABOUT RACE

1 Adapted from https://blog.prepscholar.com/race-vs-ethnicity-vs-nationality

2 Definitions from Oxford Languages.

3 https://eurweb.com/2020/12/05/the-already-tiny-group-of-
   4-black-fortune-500-ceos-loses-a-member/
4 https://www.theguardian.com/business/2021/feb/03/
   ftse-100-firms-have-no-black-executives-in-top-three-
   roles?CMP=Share_AndroidApp_Other
5 https://www.apa.org/monitor/2009/02/microaggression
6 ibid.
7 https://www.nytimes.com/article/what-is-bipoc.html
8 https://www.census.gov/quickfacts/fact/table/US/
   PST045219
9 https://www.ons.gov.uk/methodology/classificationsand
   standards/measuringequality/ethnicgroupnational
   identityandreligion
10 https://www.peoplemanagement.co.uk/experts/research/
   diversity-drives-better-decisions#:~:text=Researchers%
   20found%20that%20when%20diverse,cent%20
   improvement%20on%20decision%2Dmaking.
11 https://www.pwc.co.uk/who-we-are/annual-report/
   stories/2019/our-focus-on-ethnicity-in-workplace.html
12 https://www.nytimes.com/2020/12/01/business/dealbook/
   nasdaq-diversity-boards.html
13 https://www.theguardian.com/lifeandstyle/lostinshow
   biz/2017/apr/06/pepsi-race-luther-king-kendall-
   jenner-lindsay-lohan
14 https://www.nytimes.com/2020/08/10/podcasts/the-daily/
   cancel-culture.html?showTranscript=1
15 https://blacklivesmatter.com/herstory/

16 Definitions from Oxford Languages.

17 https://www.britannica.com/event/Jim-Crow-law

18 https://www.smithsonianmag.com/history/
where-did-term-gerrymander-come-180964118/

19 https://mashable.com/article/how-to-be-antiracist/?
europe=true

4. LISTEN TO WHAT WOMEN WANT

1 http://womenceoreport.org/

2 https://www.weforum.org/reports/gender-gap-2020-report-
100-years-pay-equality

3 https://www.pewresearch.org/fact-tank/2017/12/14/
gender-discrimination-comes-in-many-forms-for-todays-
working-women/

4 https://www.thehumancapitalhub.com/articles/How-
To-Deal-With-Gender-Bias-In-The-Workplace-

5 https://hbr.org/2016/04/if-theres-only-one-woman-in-your-
candidate-pool-theres-statistically-no-chance-shell-be-hired

6 https://edition.cnn.com/2020/08/04/business/fortune-
500-women-ceos/index.html#:~:text=The%20Fortune%
20500%20now%20has,female%20CEOs%3A%20A%20
whopping%2038

7 FTSE Women Leaders report (2020). https://www.ig.com/
uk/news-and-trade-ideas/top-female-ceos-ftse-100

8 https://commonslibrary.parliament.uk/how-much-less-were-
women-paid-in-2019/

9 https://www.catalyst.org/biascorrect/

10 https://www.hubspot.com/company-news/hubspot-named-
one-of-the-2018-best-workplaces-for-women-by-great-place-
to-work-and-fortune#:~:text=We're%20excited%20to%20
announce,diversity%20at%20HubSpot%20long%20term

11 https://girlpowermarketing.com/statistics-purchasing-
power-women/

12 https://www.americanprogress.org/issues/women/
reports/2020/10/30/492582/covid-19-sent-womens-
workforce-progress-backward/#:~:text=Four%20times%20
as%20many%20women,school%20crises%E2%80%94would%
20be%20severe

5. GET TO KNOW YOUR LGBT+ COLLEAGUES

1 https://www.forbes.com/sites/jamiewareham/2020/05/17/
map-shows-where-its-illegal-to-be-gay--30-years-since-
who-declassified-homosexuality-as-disease/?sh=
4af66258578a

2 https://eu.usatoday.com/story/money/business/2020/06/15/
supreme-court-ruling-what-does-mean-lgbt-rights-and-
where/3194423001/

3 https://www.nytimes.com/2021/01/25/us/politics/biden-
military-transgender.html

4 https://outstanding.involverolemodels.org/

5 https://hbr.org/2019/08/how-multinationals-can-help-
advance-lgbt-inclusion-around-the-world

6 https://gelawyer.com/5-examples-of-sexual-orientation-
discrimination/

7 https://www.catalyst.org/research/lesbian-gay-bisexual-and-transgender-workplace-issues/
8 https://www.stonewall.org.uk/lgbt-britain-work-report
9 Out Now (2018). https://www.outnowconsulting.com/market-reports/lgbt-diversity-show-me-the-business-case-report.aspx
10 https://www.nytimes.com/2006/01/15/magazine/the-pressure-to-cover.html
11 https://outrightinternational.org/content/acronyms-explained
12 https://www.bbc.co.uk/news/newsbeat-43042643

6. BUILD BRIDGES ACROSS GENERATIONS

1 https://mccrindle.com.au/insights/blog/gen-alpha-defined/
2 https://www.theguardian.com/society/shortcuts/2019/jan/04/move-over-millennials-and-gen-z-here-comes-generation-alpha
3 https://www.inc.com/alison-davis/instead-of-training-use-storytelling-to-build-employee-knowledge-and-address-challenges-generate-ideas-boost-teamwork.html

7. INVOLVE 100% OF EVERYONE

1 https://www.bitc.org.uk/wp-content/uploads/2019/10/bitc-wellbeing-report-mhawmentalhealthworkfullreport2019-sept2019-2.pdf
2 https://www.nami.org/mhstats
3 https://www.worldbank.org/en/topic/disability

4 https://www.worldbank.org/en/news/feature/2020/12/01/
a-more-accessible-and-sustainable-world-a-disability-
inclusive-response-to-covid-19

5 https://www.rod-group.com/insights

6 https://www.ons.gov.uk/employmentandlabourmarket/
peopleinwork/employmentandemployeetypes/datasets/
labourmarketstatusofdisabledpeoplea08

7 https://www.bls.gov/news.release/pdf/disabl.pdf

8 https://www.forbes.com/sites/cognitiveworld/2019/12/27/
neurodiversity-in-artificial-intelligence/?sh=5a4aaa24470f

9 https://www.cipd.co.uk/Images/neurodiversity-at-work_
2018_tcm18-37852.pdf

10 https://hbr.org/2017/05/neurodiversity-as-a-competitive-
advantage

11 https://www.forbes.com/sites/cognitiveworld/2019/12/
27/neurodiversity-in-artificial-intelligence/?sh=658a
314e470f

12 https://archive.acas.org.uk/neurodiversity

13 https://www.suttontrust.com/our-research/social-mobility-
in-the-workplace-an-employers-guide/

14 https://www.theladders.com/career-advice/new-data-shows-
that-going-to-an-ivy-league-school-is-no-longer-a-
requirement-for-fortune-100-ceos#:~:text=Eighty%2
Dnine%20percent%20of%20Fortune,attending%20
prestigious%20Ivy%20League%20schools

15 https://web.stanford.edu/~niederle/CEN_discrimination.pdf

16 https://fortune.com/2017/06/09/white-men-senior-
executives-fortune-500-companies-diversity-data/

8. STAY INCLUSIVE AT A DISTANCE

1 https://www.wnep.com/article/news/nation-world/remote-work-disabled-people-working-from-home/75-0b95eda7-fc29-4fc6-8713-e9a5afb9416e

2 https://www.shrm.org/hr-today/news/all-things-work/pages/the-workplace-in-2025.aspx

3 Thank you to LifeLabs, who captured this. https://explore.cultureamp.com/c/lifelabs-learning-co?x=RqMNYu

4 https://www.bloomberg.com/news/articles/2020-04-23/working-from-home-in-covid-era-means-three-more-hours-on-the-job

5 https://hrblog.spotify.com/2021/02/12/introducing-working-from-anywhere/

6 https://www.greatplacetowork.com/resources/blog/why-is-diversity-inclusion-in-the-workplace-important

9. START RECRUITING INCLUSIVELY

1 https://about.google/

2 https://www.3blmedia.com/News/Campaign/Corporate-Social-Responsibility-American-Express

3 https://www.audible.com/about/people-principles

4 https://www.tinypulse.com/blog/negative-attitudes-affect-organizational-culture

5 https://hbr.org/2020/06/how-to-design-a-better-hiring-process?registration=success

6 https://business.linkedin.com/content/dam/me/business/en-us/talent-solutions/resources/pdfs/linkedin-30-questions-to-identify-high-potential-candidates-ebook-8-7-17-uk-en.pdf

7 https://www.amazon.jobs/en/landing_pages/
interviewing-at-amazon

8 https://99designs.com/blog/marketing-advertising/
digital-marketing-trends/

10. BECOME AN ACCOMPLICE FOR DIVERSITY AND INCLUSION

1 McGregor-Smith review (2018).

2 Center for Talent Innovation (CTI, now Coqual).

3 https://www.catalyst.org/research/mentoring-necessary-
but-insufficient-for-advancement/

4 https://hbr.org/2019/02/sponsors-need-to-stop-acting-like-
mentors

5 https://www.advisoryexcellence.com/experts/steve-howe/

ACKNOWLEDGEMENTS

This book took a village and we have called extensively on the time and wisdom of the Audeliss and INvolve teams as well as our other friends and colleagues to bring this to life.

As passionate advocates for diversity and inclusion, we have laughed, fought, cried, laughed some more along the way. We are incredibly grateful to Manuel and Sherif, our respective husbands who have stood by us on this journey. These two men keep us grounded, and are always ready to give their time, energy and feedback (whether we like it or not!). The same can be said of our broader families who have enriched us with their life experience and helped to create our passion for this topic, directly or indirectly.

We thank Lucy Clayton for generously connecting us with our fantastic editor, Martina O'Sullivan. Lucy introduced us to this universe, and she and her partner, Steve Haines, were invaluable in getting us off the starting blocks.

Martina has been truly phenomenal in her support and patience as we navigated this new adventure and was exactly the person we needed to keep us on track alongside our ridiculously busy day jobs. Mark Griffiths helped to bring order to our jumble of thoughts and ideas on the topic and our copyeditor, Sarah-Jane Forder, then pulled everything into line further. This team was truly exceptional and, as we have just experienced the most hectic year of our professional lives in the midst of this effort, they really did a great job of keeping us on task and maintaining a strong relationship throughout.

We mentioned the broader team but wanted to extend particular thanks to Ryan Vincent and Justin Firth, who invested heavily in supporting the content creation and messaging and ensuring that we remained current and embodied the right tone. In a space where the language and perspectives are changing by the day, if not by the hour, Ryan and Justin did an exceptional job of supporting us in taking a progressive view and ensuring that we were consistently communicating in a way that would best connect with our readers (we hope you agree!). Kim Robinson also requires a special shout-out for reviewing our race chapter and making sure that there was authenticity that appropriately represented some of the narrative we have seen in the wake of the Black Lives Matter movement.

A cornerstone of this book is the contributions that we were able to secure from the CEOs who gave their time and put themselves out there as outspoken advocates. So a special thank you to:

• Greg Case at Aon

• Keith Barr at IHG

• David Kenny at Nielsen

• Alan Jope at Unilever

• Marc Benioff at Salesforce

- Jim Fitterling at Dow

- Richard Branson at Virgin Group

- Andy Briggs at Phoenix Group

- Ron O'Hanley at State Street

- Denis Machuel at Sodexo

- Don Katz at Audible

Beyond the core team and the CEOs we connected with, we have reached out to numerous friends for their thoughts and input and would like to thank Hugh Tallents for being a well-informed and progressive straight white guy who doesn't mind speaking his truth and bringing his sharp professional opinion to bear on tone and voice.

We also want to thank each other for making this dream a reality through hard work and determination. We did it and we are super-happy with the end result. We hope that *How to Get Your Act Together* will help drive the change we need to see in business to build more diverse and inclusive workplaces globally.